WY PLAY HOUSE

Off Camera

By **Marcia Layne**

Director **Femi Elufowoju, jr**
Designer **Joanna Parker**
Lighting Designer **Malcolm Rippeth**
Sound Designer **Mic Pool**
DSM **Sarah Northcott**

First performance of this production:
Courtyard Theatre, West Yorkshire Playhouse,
27 June 2003

West Yorkshire Playhouse
Quarry Hill
Leeds
LS2 7UP
www.wyp.org.uk

The Company

Maxine Burth Anisha
Llewella Gideon Sandra
Johann Myers Passion
Yvette Rochester Duncan Babs
Seun Shote Ras Simi

Production Thanks
Wray and Nephew
BDF Beiersdorf UK Ltd. for the Nivea Sun Lotion
Jamaican Tourist Board
Charles Wells Brewery Ltd. for the Red Stripe

BSL Interpreted performance
Tuesday 8 July 7.45pm
BSL Interpreter
Alan Haythornthwaite

Audio Described performances
Thursday 10 July 2.30pm
Friday 11 July 7.45pm
Audio Describers
Anne Muers and Madeline Irwin

There will be no interval for this performance.

Smoking in the auditorium is not permitted. Please ensure that mobile phones, pagers and digital alarm watches are SWITCHED OFF before you enter the auditorium.

Cast

Maxine Burth Anisha

Trained: Rose Bruford College. Theatre credits include: *A Caribbean Abroad* (Library Theatre, Manchester); *Shoot 2 Win* (Theatre Royal, Stratford East); *How To Free Your Bitch* (Black Theatre Co-operative); *A Raisin In The Sun* (Green Room, Inner Manchester); *Wicked Game, All The Helicopter Night* (West Yorkshire Playhouse); *Handicap Race* (Salisbury Playhouse); *Translations* (Half Moon Theatre); *Song Of An Honorary Soulman* (Smilin' Mongoose); *Stamping, Shouting, Singing Home* (Theatre Royal, Northampton); *No Mean Street* (Red Ladder Theatre); *And Here Comes A Candle* (Inner City); *A Midsummer Nights Dream, Othello, The Lady From The Sea* (The Barn). Television credits include: *Doctors, Blue Murder, Bullying, 73 Million To One, Playing The Field, Emmerdale, Always And Everyone, Wilmot, Coronation Street, Big Meg Little Meg, Liverpool One, The Bill, Hetty Wainthropp Investigates, Out Of The Blue, Cardiac Arrest, Lost For Words, Band Of Gold, For Amusement Only, House Of Windsor, Medics, Elidor, Own Goal*. Film credits include: *Eulogy, Girls Night, Kisko – A Life For A Life, Deadly Voyage, Heart*.

Llewella Gideon Sandra

Theatre credits include: *The Sunshine Boys* (Tour); *Holiday* (Duchess Theatre); *Blues Brother Soul Sisters, The Amen Corner* (Bristol Old Vic); *Temporary Rupture, Bitter And Twisted* (Black Theatre Co-Operative). Television credits include: *The Crouches, TLC, Fifteen Stories High, Juggling, Ur Here, The Big Smoke, Big Train, Porkpie, EastEnders, Murder Most Horrid, Absolutely Fabulous, The Real McCoy*. Film credits include: *Spice The Movie, Dollars*. Radio credits include: *Unspoken* (BBC Radio Manchester), *Little Big Woman, Emerald Green, Women's Hour* (BBC Radio Four); *Borderline, Behind The Couch* (BBC Radio Five), *Lenny Henry Show* (BBC Radio One). Writing credits include: *Fruit Salad* (debuted May 2003)

Seun Shote Ras Simi

Trained: Manchester Metropolitan University. Theatre credits include: *Blue Orange* (Duchess Theatre); *The Amazing Birthday* (Polka Theatre); *The Importance Of Being Earnest* (Albany Theatre); *Breaking The Ice* (Pop-Up Theatre); *Inside Out* (Theatre Venture); *Tickets & Ties* (Theatre Royal, Stratford East/Tour). Television credits include: *40, Trail of Guilt, The Bill, The Many Cinderellas, The Slot: Maths Mysteries, Faith In The Future, Common As Muck*. Radio credits include: *Evaristo's Epitaph, A Day In The Life Ivan Denisovitch* and *Homeboys* (BBC Radio Four).

Johann Myers Passion

Theatre credits include: *Ragamuffin* (Tour); *Moon On A Rainbow Shawl* (Nottingham Playhouse/Tour); *No Sweat* (Birmingham Rep); *Behsheram* (Birmingham Rep/Soho Theatre); *Drag On* (Royal Court) *Someone Who'll Watch Over Me* (Next Stage Theatre Company); *God's Door* (Nottingham Playhouse); *Christie In Love* (First Floor Theatre Company). Television credits include: *State Of Play, Buried, The Bill, Casualty, Kavanagh QC, The Token King, Soldier Soldier, The Locksmith.* Film credits include: *One For The Road, Highbinders, South Kensington, Black Hawk Down, Kiss Kiss Bang Bang, Lava, Blood, A Room For Romeo Brass, Twenty Four Seven.*

Yvette Rochester Duncan Babs

Theatre credits include: *Fruit Salad* (Greenwich Theatre); *Funny Black Women On The Edge* (Theatre Royal, Stratford East); *Incompatibly Yours* (Pegasus Theatre/The Lyric, Hammersmith); *The Thing About Shirley, Sunday Selection* (Hackney Empire); *Getting Any* (National Black Theatre Festival, North Carolina); *Roy Diamond Laughter Lounge* (Tricycle Theatre); *Sisters* (Riverside Studios); *Amen Corner* (Bristol Old Vic); Funny Black Women On The Edge (Theatre Royal, Stratford East/Tour); *Small Offers* (Yaw Asantawa Arts Centre); *Children On The Edge* (London Palladium); *Cinderella* (Hackney Empire/Shepherds Bush Empire); *Taking Charge (*The Drill Hall); *Night Nurse* (Shaw Theatre/ Hackney Empire/Lewisham Theatre) *Princess Black* (The Cave, Birmingham/Shaw Theatre). Television and Film credits include: *Flava, Club Class, Touching Evil, Get Up Stand Up, Chef, Devon Dozen, Princess Black.* Radio credits include: *Sharp Cuts, Angie Le Mar's Comedy Jam, Sunshine Airways.*

Creatives

Marcia Layne Writer

Coventry born Marcia currently lives in Sheffield, since completing a degree at Sheffield Hallam University, majoring in English and Media studies. Her first play *Sister Esteem* was written in 2000 for Ticket To Write, which was a joint initiative between Paines Plough and the West Yorkshire Playhouse. She has worked as an Arts Officer for five years and is a member of PALM, a creative writing group for Black women, based in Huddersfield. In the past, she has contributed to *Sheffield City Press*, regional magazine *Cooldown* and was the editor of Black Student magazine *Pyramid. Off Camera* was originally commissioned by Paines Plough for Wild Lunch VI at the Young Vic and is Marcia's first full length play. She is currently working on her first novel *A Mother's Tale* and her next play *Legacy.*

Femi Elufowoju, jr Director

Femi Elufowoju, jr trained at Bretton Hall. As an actor, Femi has worked with some of the country's leading theatre directors including seasons with Oxford Stage Company, Talawa, the Royal Court, Royal National Theatre, Theatre de Complicite and West Yorkshire Playhouse. Femi has recorded over a hundred radio plays for the BBC including two series on *Linda Smith's Brief Guide to Time-wasting* and playing Mohammed Ali on the popular *Mark Steel Lecture* series for BBC Radio Four. He has also recently joined the cast of *Westway*, BBC World Service's favourite soap opera. Femi's television credits include *The Knock II* and Lynda La Plante's *Supply and Demand*. His last screen appearance was in the critically acclaimed feature film *The Legend of 1900*, alongside Tim Roth and Peter Vaughan, directed by Oscar award-winning director Giuseppe Tornatore. His career as a theatre director commenced in 1995 with *Acquisitive Case* at the Southwark Playhouse followed by a year at the Theatre Royal, Stratford East in 1996 under Philip Hedley. He is the founder and Artistic Director of Tiata Fahodzi. Productions for Tiata Fahodzi include *Booked!, Bonded, Makinde* and *Abyssinia*. As a freelance director, Femi recently directed Patrick Marber's *Dealer's Choice* for the Salisbury Playhouse and is currently Associate Director (trainee) at the Royal Court in London and Associate Director (courtesy of Esmée Fairbairn Foundation) at West Yorkshire Playhouse.

Joanna Parker Designer

Her set and costume designs for theatre include: *Dealer's Choice* at the Salisbury Playhouse; *An Immaculate Misconception* at the Bridewell Theatre; *My Matisse* at the 2002 Edinburgh Fringe; *Apache Tears* with Clean Break Theatre Company; *The Suicide* at the Beckett Centre in Dublin, Schiller's *The Robbers* at the Gate, Martin Crimp's new version of *The Misanthrope*, David Mamet's *American Buffalo* at the Young Vic, George Walker's *Featuring Loretta*, the costumes for *Nabokov's Gloves* and the première of Timberlake Wertenbaker's *After Darwin* at Hampstead. For opera and music theatre her designs include: *The Noise of Time* – Theatre de Complicite with the Emerson String Quartet at the Lincoln Center, New York, the Barbican Centre London and European Festivals; the costumes for *Friend of the People* at Scottish Opera directed by Christopher Alden, set and costumes for Handel's *Gulio Cesare* for the Royal Opera House at Shaftesbury Theatre; Janacek's The *Cunning Little Vixen* (also for English Touring Opera), Smetana's *The Kiss* and Handel's *Flavio* for Opera Theatre Company in Dublin and European tour, a site specific design at the Corn Exchange, Cambridge for *Heroes Don't Dance*, a newly commissioned Royal Opera House community project and Schoenberg's *Pierrot Lunaire* for the Knack at the ENO Works, *Masquerade* for the Guildhall School for Music and Drama. Future designs include: *A Midsummer Night's Dream* and *The Marriage of Figaro* for English Touring Opera.

Malcolm Rippeth Lighting Designer

Theatre credits include: *John Gabriel Borkman* and *Anton Chekhov* (English Touring Theatre); *Dealer's Choice* (Salisbury Playhouse); *Bintou* (Arcola); *The Snow Queen, Noir* and *The Tiger's Bride* (Northern Stage); *Pandora's Box* (national tour for Northern Stage and Kneehigh); *Foyer* and *The Selfish Giant* (Haymarket Theatre, Leicester); *Abyssinia* (national tour for Tiata Fahodzi); *Tear from a Glass Eye* (Gate Theatre/RNT Studio); *The Old Curiosity Shop* (Southwark Playhouse); *A Billion Seconds* (national tour for Strathcona Theatre Company); *Three Wishes, A Supercollider for the Family, Poppy Day* and *My Last Week with Modola* (Pleasance, Edinburgh); *Bob Downe – Whiter! Brighter!* (Assembly Rooms, Edinburgh); *Mel and Sue – Back to Our Roots* (national tour); *The Woolgatherer* (BAC); *Average White Girl – Reconstructed* (British Festival of Visual Theatre); *Spitting Love* (New Writing North); *Cooking With Elvis* (Live Theatre, Newcastle). Opera credits include: *Who Put Bella in the Wych Elm* and *Infinito Nero* (Almeida Aldeburgh Opera). Dance credits include: *The Ball* (national and European tour for balletLORENT).

Mic Pool Sound Designer

In a twenty-six year career in theatre sound Mic has been resident at The Lyric Hammersmith, the Royal Court, Tyne Theatre Company and toured internationally with Ballet Rambert. He has designed the sound for over 300 productions including more than 150 for the West Yorkshire Playhouse where he is currently Director of Creative Technology. He received a TMA award in 1992 for Best Designer (Sound) for *Life Is A Dream* and was nominated for both the Lucille Lortel and the Drama Desk Award for Outstanding Sound Design 2001 for the New York production of *The Unexpected Man*. Recent theatre credits include: *Brand* (RSC/Haymarket Theatre); *Pretending To Be Me* (West Yorkshire Playhouse/West End); *Art* (West End, Broadway and worldwide); *Shockheaded Peter* (Cultural Industry world tour/West End); *The Unexpected Man* (West End/Broadway); *Another Country* (Arts Theatre); *My Dad's Corner Shop* (Derby Playhouse); *Dead Funny* (Nottingham Playhouse); *Hijra* (Bush Theatre/Plymouth Theatre Royal/West Yorkshire Playhouse); *A Midsummer Night's Dream, The Seagull, Victoria, Romeo and Juliet, Twelfth Night* and *The Late Shakespeare Plays* at the Roundhouse (RSC); *The Seagull, The Tempest, Naked Justice, Broken Glass, Inconceivable, Johnson Over Jordan, Dangerous Corner, Eden End, Horse & Carriage, The Lady in the Van, Rosencrantz and Guildenstern are Dead, Hamlet, Larkin With Women, Pretending to be Me, Four Nights in Knaresborough, The Accrington Pals, A Small Family Business* (West Yorkshire Playhouse); *Smoking With Lulu* (West Yorkshire Playhouse/Soho Theatre, London). Video work for theatre includes: *The Wizard of Oz, Johnson Over Jordan* (West Yorkshire Playhouse); *Dangerous Corner* (West Yorkshire Playhouse/West End); *Singin' In The Rain* (West Yorkshire Playhouse/Royal National Theatre/ national tour); *The Turk In Italy, Il Trovatore* (ENO); *The Ring Cycle* (New National Theatre Tokyo); *Il Tabarro* (WNO Max); *Dr Jekyll and Mr Hyde* (West Yorkshire Playhouse Schools Company). Television credits include: Sound design for *How Wide Is Your Sky?* (Channel 4).

ARTS FOR ALL AT THE WEST YORKSHIRE PLAYHOUSE

Since opening in 1990, the West Yorkshire Playhouse has established a reputation both nationally and internationally as one of Britain's most exciting and active producing theatres – winning awards for everything from its productions to its customer service. The Playhouse provides both a thriving focal point for the communities of West Yorkshire and theatre of the highest standard for audiences throughout the region and beyond. It produces up to 16 of its own shows each year in its two auditoria and stages over 1000 performances, workshops, readings and community events, watched by over 250,000 people.

Alongside its work on stage the Playhouse has an expansive and groundbreaking programme of education and community initiatives. As well as a busy foyer and restaurant which are home to a range of activities through the week, the Playhouse offers extensive and innovative education programmes for children and adults, a wide range of unique community projects and is engaged in the development of culturally diverse art and artists. It is this 'Arts for All' environment, as well as a high profile portfolio of international theatre, new writing for the stage and major productions with leading artists that has kept the Playhouse constantly in the headlines and at the forefront of the arts scene.

Conference, Catering and Bar
Steven Whitaker Catering and Commercial Manager
Sandra Gaffigan Deputy Catering Manager
Charles Smith Head Chef
Louise Poulter Chef de Partie
Michael Montgomery Sous Chef
Simon Armitage and **Linda Monaghan** Commis Chefs
Lee Moran, Chris Hill, Callum Stewart and **Lee Dennell** Kitchen Porters
Caron Hawley and **Esther Lewis** Kitchen Assistants
Diana Kendall Restaurant Supervisor
Kath Langton and **Gemma Voller** Restaurant Assistants
Sarah Allen, Charlene Kendall, Victoria Burt, Sharisse Ghoneim, Ruth Baxter, Jimmy Dunbar, Emma Harrison, Jessica Best, Lee Dennell, Wayne Gregory and **Emma Witherland** Catering Assistants*
Malcolm Salsbury Bar Manager
Sally Thomas and **Jennie Webster** Assistant Bar Managers
Victoria Hemsley, Marion Miller, Francis Ratcliff, Sophie Pearson, Graeme Thompson, Pamela Wilson, Laura Wilks and **Jo Ash** Bar Assistants*

Company and Stage Management
Diane Asken Company Manager
Paul Veysey and **Karen Whitting** Stage Managers
Hannah Lobb and **Sarah Northcott** Deputy Stage Managers
Sarah Braybook and **Christine Guthrie** Assistant Stage Managers

Customer Services
Kathy Dean, Jackie Gascoigne and **Rachel Blackeby**

Finance
Teresa Garner Finance Manager
Coleen Anderson Finance Officer
Jenny Copley Cashier
Sadie Bostridge Payroll Officer
Fran Major Ledger Clerk

Housekeeping
Mary Ambrose, Eddy Dube, Michaela Singleton, Paul Robinson, Teresa Singleton, Sarah Wonnacott and **Mike Hilton** Cleaners*

Maintenance
Frank Monaghan Maintenance Manager
Jim Gaffigan and **Martin McHugh** Maintenance Assistants
Shane Montgomery General Services Assistant

Marketing and Sales
Nick Boaden Marketing Manager
Angela Robertson Sales Manager
Duncan Grant Graphic Design Manager
Sarah Kennedy Senior Marketing Officer
Simon Bedford Marketing Officer
Aimee Green Graphic Design Officer*
Caroline Gornall Deputy Sales Manager
Lynn Hudson, Mel Worman and **Bronia Daniels** Duty Supervisors
Caroline Dennis, Maureen Kirkby, Sally Thomas, Pene Hayward, Sarah Jennings, Rachael Margrave, Sally Mackay, Lucy Hird, Dena Marsh and **Tom Stoker** Box Office Assistants

New Writing
Alex Chisholm Literary and Events Manager
Clare Duffy Pearson Writer in Residence
Anita Franklin BBC Writer in Residence

Paint Shop
Virginia Whiteley Head Scenic Artist
Brian Van Der Heever and **Sarah East** Freelance Scenic Artists

Performance Staff
Andy Charlesworth and **Jon Murray** Firemen
Rebecca Ashdown, Nathanya Laurent, Shaun Exley, Simon Howarth, Sally McKay, Hayley Mort, Jo Murray, Soazig Nicholson, Genevieve Say, Jamie Steer, Daneill Whyles, Jemal Cohen, Rachel Blakeby, Sangeeta Chana, Indy Panesar, Marcus Stewart, Andrew Ashdown, Simon Biggins, Avril Fredericks, Sophie Goodeve, Deborah Hargreave, Fiona Heseltine, Kimberley Hughes, Monisha Roy, Lewis Smith, Lucy Stenhouse, Holly Thomas, Darrelle

Villa, **Rebeka Wilkes**, **Tom Stoker**,
Leigh Exley, **Charmaine Jenkins** and
William Shirley Attendants*
Jamie Steer and **Sarah Jennings**
Playhouse Hosts*

Press
Rachel Coles Head of Press
Stacey Arnold Press Officer

Production Electricians
Stephen Sinclair Chief Electrician
Christopher Sutherland Acting
Deputy Chief Electrician
Drew Wallis and **Melani Nicola**
Electricians
Deborah Joyce Temporary Electrician
Benoit Dupraz Work Placement

Production Management
Suzi Cubbage Production Manager
Eddie de Pledge Production Manager
Christine Alcock Production
Administrator

Props Department
Chris Cully Head of Props
Scott Thompson, **Susie Cockram**
and **Sarah Partridge** Prop Makers

Schools Touring Company
Gail McIntyre Director
Ysanne-Marie Morton Touring and
Projects Co-ordinator
Sara Bienvenu, **Eve Robertson** and
Nick Stanley Actors
Marc Walton Technical Assistant
Capucine Marilly Stage Management
Work Placement*

Security
Denis Bray and **Darkside Security**

Sound Department
Glen Massam Chief Sound Technician
Martin Pickersgill Acting Deputy
Sound Technician

Technical Stage Management
Martin Ross Technical Stage Manager
Michael Cassidy Deputy Technical
Stage Manager
Julian Brown and **Chris Harrison**
Stage Technicians

Theatre Operations
Helen Child Head of Operations
Karen Johnson Theatre Manager
Sheila Howarth, **Jeni Douglas**,
Jonathan Dean and **Tom Stoker** Duty
Managers*
Faisal Mahmood Fast Track
Placement

Wardrobe Department
Stephen Snell Head of Wardrobe
Victoria Marzetti Deputy Head of
Wardrobe
Julie Ashworth Head Cutter
Selina Nightingale Cutter
Alison Barrett Costume Prop Maker/
Dyer
Catherine Lowe and **Nicole Martin**
Wardrobe Assistants
Anne-Marie Hewitt Costume Hire
Manager
Kim Freeland Wig and Make-up
Supervisor
Catherine Newton Wardrobe
Maintenance / Head Dresser

*Denotes part-time

West Yorkshire Playhouse Corporate Supporters

Sponsors of the Arts Development Unit

Production Sponsors

A Small Family Business

DIRECTORS CLUB

Executive Level Members

Associate Level Members

YORKSHIRE POST

Director Level Members

Baker Tilly
Bank of Scotland
BWD Rensburg
Crowne Plaza Leeds
David Yablon
GNER
GVA Grimley
Hiscox

New Horizons
Pinsent Curtis Biddle
Provident Financial
The BWB Partnership
Thompson Design
Yorkshire Dales Ice Cream
Yorkshire Television

One Performance Sponsors

Little Shop of Horrors

If you would like to learn how your organisation can become involved with the success of the West Yorkshire Playhouse please contact the Corporate Affairs Department on 0113 213 7275 or email networking@wyp.org.uk

WY PLAY HOUSE

THE DIRECTORS CLUB CREATIVE NETWORKING

THE DIRECTORS CLUB

Looking for a refreshingly alternative way to entertain clients and reward staff? The Directors Club brings the excitement and glamour of the theatre to you in four simple packages. Cost from £1000 (ex vat).

CREATIVE NETWORKING

Creative Networking helps you to promote your business, reach a new audience and train your staff – all in a truly creative way. For more information on Creative Networking and our conference facilities, call Kate Jeeves on 0113 213 7275 or email networking@wyp.org.uk

First published in 2003 by Oberon Books Ltd.
(incorporating Absolute Classics)
521 Caledonian Road, London N7 9RH
Tel: 020 7607 3637 / Fax: 020 7607 3629

e-mail: oberon.books@btinternet.com
www.oberonbooks.com

A catalogue record for this book is available from the
British Library.

ISBN: 1 84002 381 3

Printed in Great Britain by Antony Rowe Ltd, Chippenham.

Dedicated to my sisters Jackie 'Avanda J' Layne,
Carol Layne and my sister in spirit, Marcia Griffiths
and
My nephews Reuben, Joshua, Meshaq and Jeremiah

'Let not what you cannot do tear from your
hands what you can' *Ashanti proverb*

Acknowledgements

I give thanks to the Most High, first and foremost, who makes all things possible.

Much love to the many people who have encouraged me and believed in me on this journey. Blessings to Carol (ashé), Ras Marce, you taught me with love comes acceptance. George Matheson, my most relentless supporter, I believe in you too. Phil James, Sol B River (am I forgiven?) Robert Pitt, Courttia Newland, Rod Adams, Vinnie Spears (I can't forget), Michelle McCelland, Michelle Odudu, Samina, Avanda, Susi & Sam (I would feel a way!). Dave Carvill, my best friend. You loved me when I thought no one else did. Thank you for always being there. Reverend Jackee Holder, you've been a constant inspiration. I'm honoured to call you my friend.

To my sistas at PALM, Amanda, Andrea, Ann, Cherean, Everlyn, Louise, Lydia, Rosanna and Sharmain my soul sista. I've missed you all. Keep writing.

And to the rest of the Huddersfield krew who have my back, thank you. You know who you are.

Thanks to all at West Yorkshire Playhouse and Paines Plough and the three wonderful casts who have performed *Off Camera*.

Last but not least, much love to my extended family in Jamaica. In particular, thank you Delton for taking such good care of me and for giving me bear joke. I've never laughed so much.

Characters

ANISHA BROWN

BABS (BRENDA) COLE

RAS SIMI

PASSION

SANDRA

Note
The following playscript went to print while the play was still in rehearsal and may differ slightly from the play as performed.

Scene 1

There are two beds side by side (possibly horizontally so you can barely see one, beyond the other), one is occupied, with light bedding covering it from head to toe. There is an electric fan blowing cold air across both beds. The woman in bed (ANISHA) has her back to BABS who is bent over her suitcase, selecting clothes. ANISHA seems agitated, sleeping but restlessly. BABS, who is wearing a short nightshirt, picks out bikinis and holds them up against herself. The radio is on very low and she turns it up slightly as a new tune starts that she particularly likes ('No Letting Go' – Wayne Wonder) and checks over her shoulder to see if she has disturbed ANISHA. When it has no effect on her friend, she turns it up a little more, posing in the mirror with her bikinis and playfully moving to the diwali rhythm as if she is performing to an audience. She soon has the desired effect (a combination of the music and her clapping) and ANISHA wakes, turns and stares at her.

ANISHA: (*Little vex.*) A wha do yu gyal?

BABS: (*Brightly.*) Marning.

ANISHA: Already?

BABS: Isn't this great? Last week I was trying to decide whether to pay the phone bill or my visa card and now (*Holds a bikini bottom up to her front and models for ANISHA.*) ...Is it the red one or the blue?

ANISHA: At least pick one with a batty.

BABS: Why?

ANISHA: Why, cause you'll come like the pied piper the minute you step outside. Bear man on your case.

BABS: (*Liking the idea.*) And that's a problem because?

ANISHA: Have you forgotten why you're here?

BABS: It's good to keep a man on his toes.

17

ANISHA: And what makes you think he won't then keep you on yours?

BABS: (*Pauses then selects another costume.*) Mmmm, I suppose you're right but I do quite like the attention though.

ANISHA: But you said they don't need much encouragement.

BABS: True, I could be wearing a black sack with knock knee and cross eye and still have them calling – (*Adopts accent.*) Hey inglis, me like yuh, yuh no baby.

ANISHA: Maybe that's taking it too far.

BABS: Yuh tink lie me a tell? Watch and learn.

ANISHA: Well they can look but they better not even think about touching.

BABS: (*Kisses her teeth.*) You can be so closed off sometimes, you need to loosen up a bit man.

ANISHA: Like I did with Darren.

BABS: That's what I don't get about you, you either write men off completely or you see the ones who are totally inappropriate.

ANISHA: (*Defensively.*) That's not true.

BABS: Are you trying to prove to yourself there are no good ones out there?

ANISHA: I thought that was your mission in life.

BABS: No, I find good ones, they just don't always feel the same way about me…you dated the crackhead?

ANISHA: How was I to know? He just seemed a bit vulnerable.

BABS: Is that what made him pocket the tip you left at the restaurant? Or steal your DVD player?

ANISHA: I can't prove that was him.

BABS casts her a look of disbelief.

It was a mistake, *we* all make them.

BABS: What are you implying?

ANISHA: You met Passion the rebound.

BABS: I was over Kelvin.

ANISHA: Really? Yet the minute he announced his engagement you jumped on a plane.

BABS: You can be over a man but it still pisses you off when they meet someone before you do.

ANISHA: So you admit there was a little score settling going on.

BABS: Not at all. I was ready to meet someone though and there's a shortage of men in England.

ANISHA: You mean the best ones have been taken.

BABS: I read it in a magazine. One in four black men date white women and only one in seven black women date white men. It came from the census.

ANISHA: You know, when they start quoting the census, why don't they tell us something useful, like which men are still single, where they live and how much they earn?

BABS: Belive. Knowing you, you would still freeze them out. Because I know how you stay I've done you a favour. You remember Simi, our driver from the other night…?

ANISHA: (*Cuts in.*) Of course I remember. I told you already, he's not my type. (*Beckoning to the table.*) Pass the insect repellent.

BABS: (*Deadpan.*) That ain't gonna work. (*Hands over the bottle.*)

ANISHA offers her a false smile and sprays her arms, legs and torso.

ANISHA: Something is irritating me.

BABS: He's cool, believe me and genuine. Give him a bly, man.

ANISHA: He's a rasta…

BABS: He's righteous.

ANISHA: How do I know he's not a rent-a-dread?

BABS: Well, don't rent him.

ANISHA: If only it were that simple.

BABS: Passion says you have to watch the ones who spend day and night on the beach, don't have no job and just run down tourists twenty-four-seven.

Upstage, PASSION, a man in his mid-twenties appears with a rake, accompanied by the faint sound of music. He has short hair, is wearing a Nike visor and is dressed casually in low-hanging knee-length denim shorts, shorts showing beneath, with a white rag hanging out the back pocket. He's also wearing a sleeveless t-shirt or string vest. He's wearing name brand trainers. He rakes half-heartedly while moving in a mildly provocative way to the music and occasionally he hails to someone or watches a passer-by. This overlaps with the remainder of this action.

ANISHA: (*Sarcastically.*) Oh well if Passion says…

BABS: (*Defensively.*) What do you mean by that?

ANISHA: Well they're friends, aren't they?

BABS: He was talking generally at the time. Once you're here a little while you'll be able to spot them for yourself and you'll realise Simi ain't like that. I'm not trying to twist your arm or anything but I've asked him to pick you up later.

ANISHA: You've done what?

BABS: I'm not letting you spend another day hiding in the room.

ANISHA: I'm not hiding, I've been thinking.

BABS: About what?

ANISHA: Just thinking. And I'm well tired.

BABS: Jet lag?

ANISHA: I don't know. Probably. I just need to wind down.

BABS: I've noticed you've been tossing and turning a lot. You been having bad dreams or sumting? You called out last night?

ANISHA: (*Cagily.*) What did I say?

BABS: (*Breathing heavily.*) Simi oh Simi… (*Starts laughing.*)

ANISHA: Yeah right, I think you were dreaming.

BABS: No seriously, I heard you but I'm not sure what you said.

ANISHA: I'll be having nightmares if you don't call off this date.

BABS: I can't. He's busy all day running a tour. He'll be back around four-thirty and then he's coming straight for you.

ANISHA: Does he have a phone?

BABS: I don't know the number.

ANISHA: You can get it though.

BABS: (*Pauses.*) Look, what's the big deal, it's one afternoon? He's safe honestly. I think if you just give him a chance, you'll like him.

ANISHA: (*Smiling suddenly.*) How badly do you want me to go?

BABS: Why you a show me teet?

ANISHA: How badly? (*Stretches out upturned palm.*)

BABS: (*Mock disbelief.*) A wha dis? Yuh wan me to grease your palm? You catch on quick...

ANISHA: (*Laughing.*) If you paid me would that make you my pimp?

BABS: No, it would mek me a rars idyat.

ANISHA: No change there then... Look I'll go but if I don't like him...

BABS: That's the end of that, he's a big man. Don't burn your bridges though, he's one of the good ones.

ANISHA: I don't know why you ain't with him yourself.

BABS: (*Proudly.*) I got the other good one.

ANISHA: (*Cautiously.*) Passion seems nice...

BABS: He is.

ANISHA: ...but I can't see what you two have in common...well, other than he works on the beach and you're staying on the beach.

BABS: (*Suggestively.*) We have a little bit more than that.

ANISHA: Okay, you don't have to go there again. (*Holds up one hand as BABS is poised to speak.*) ...I meant beyond the physical.

BABS: Oh. (*Pauses.*) Well, of course we've done all kinds together.

As BABS and ANISHA are talking, PASSION moves across the stage and sits in one of three cinema seats. He sits slouched low with his legs spread wide apart.

ANISHA: Like…

BABS smiles at some distant memory.

(*Dryly.*) The suspense is killing me.

BABS picks up a tray of nachos and two paper cups with lids and straws and makes her way over to PASSION. The light dims on ANISHA and goes up on PASSION. As BABS makes her way down the aisle in the auditorium, it's obvious she has limited space and is apologetic as she passes each person en route to PASSION and is a little flustered as a result. She has to pass PASSION to sit on his right and he is a little slow moving his legs.

BABS: Sorry…excuse me…sorry…sorry.

PASSION: Yuh tek long, man.

Takes the nachos and one drink and begins crunching and slurping loudly. BABS nudges him.

Me nah hav no manners, tanks baby.

Resumes crunching and slurping. BABS rolls her eyes.

BABS: (*Whisper.*) Passion!

PASSION: Wha du yu? Yu wan?

PASSION offers nachos, BABS refuses and the overhead lights dim and the cinema screen lights up in front of them.

VOICE: Can you all please rise for the Jamaican National anthem.

BABS is a bit self-conscious and looks to her right and behind her (to check if others are standing), before she gets to her feet. PASSION continues eating and drinking obliviously as if he hasn't heard. The opening bars of the National Anthem are heard before BABS notices PASSION hasn't moved and she pulls him to his feet. He still has food in his hand.

BABS: (*Whispers.*) You should put that down.

PASSION: Chuh. (*Places food on the seat behind him.*)

A mobile phone rings behind them and a male voice is heard speaking a few rows behind. PASSION turns and kisses his teeth.

BABS: That's well disrespectful.

One second after BABS speaks another phone starts to ring – ringtone Beenie Man – 'Red Red Red'. It rings for a little while before BABS realises it's his.

(*Whispers.*) Passion!

PASSION: (*Answers the phone quietly.*) Yes? (*Looking vex.*) Wha do yu?

Theres a lengthy pause and PASSION looks increasingly agitated and his voice gets louder as a result.

Me tell yu aready, me nah have it. (*Short pause. Kisses his teeth.*) Yu done no ow it go. (*Short pause.*) Lissen me, me cyarn tark now…later. (*Hangs up the phone.*)

During the call, BABS tries to distance herself and eventually sits in her seat. When PASSION finishes speaking he pulls her to her feet.

PASSION: How yu fe do dat?

As the anthem finishes PASSION sits down and BABS remains standing.

Yu can sit down now.

BABS: I'm going to the ladies.

PASSION looks confused. BABS speaks in patois.

To da bartroom.

PASSION: Go and come.

As BABS begins to make her way, PASSION calls to her.

PASSION: Babs.

BABS: Umm?

PASSION: Get me a nex one of dese. (*Holds up his nacho tray.*) And bring sum black pepper come.

He can see she is reluctant so he gives her a large, sexy smile and she visibly softens and smiles back.

Tanks baby.

BABS: No problem.

BABS makes her way back to ANISHA and PASSION returns to the beach bar.

ANISHA: First time in a cinema?

BABS nods.

And you went to see Lord of the Rings?

BABS: (*In patois.*) Lawd of de rings. When the fighting started, he was criss.

ANISHA: There ain't no black people in that film. If you ask me it's racist, portraying a world without blacks with one blue eyed boy to save the day.

BABS: (*Deadpan.*) Save it, we're on holiday. What time is it? (*Reaches for watch.*)

ANISHA: Time you woke up and took off the blinkers.

BABS: Shit, I've gotta go, I'm meeting Cynthia for breakfast. She's going to show me her ring.

ANISHA: Frodo gave her the ring?

BABS: Didn't I tell you? Cyrus asked her to marry him. He made the ring himself.

ANISHA: What from, bamboo and rockstone?

BABS: I don't know yet. Why you so cynical?

ANISHA: Why? Because the pair of you sound like a couple of stellas? You've known these guys five minutes and rather than just getting your groove back and done, you're treating this holiday shit like it's real.

BABS: I'll 'low you that because it's your first time but you'll change your tune by the end of the trip. I guarantee it. Anyway Cynthia's known her man a year at least. She used to fly here from DC for long weekends til she moved here last month for a six month stay, so your five minutes is way off.

ANISHA: It's just a figure of speech. You know the deal.

BABS: …And for the record, Stella also got married.

ANISHA: Damn, Terry McMillan has a lot to answer for.

Scene 2

Fade to blackout as the faint ragga music accompanying PASSION and light fades up on the beach scene. Enter RAS SIMI, a man in his late-twenties with shoulder-length dreadlocks, wearing loose fitting combat style trousers, short sleeved cotton shirt and Timberland boots. He's drinking from a plastic bottle and looks hot and tired. He is striding like a man on a mission and doesn't see PASSION until he calls to him.

PASSION: Ras!

RAS SIMI nods to PASSION and walks over. They touch fists.

RAS SIMI: Blessed.

PASSION: W'happen bredrin? Yu a drop foot like yu turn English man aready.

RAS SIMI: (*Smiles.*) Me deh pon a fars move. Fram marning I shoulda reach Mayfield Falls wid two American girl.

PASSION: So wha?

RAS SIMI: Sleep me a sleep.

PASSION: Yu hav money fe dash way?

RAS SIMI: (*Loudly.*) No sah! Me a look fe dem right now.

PASSION: Two blonde gyal fram Texas, stay ova so? (*Beckons with head.*)

RAS SIMI: Mmm, so dem say.

PASSION: Yes, mi see di strong looking one, big up so. (*Indicates large chest.*) Dem garn wid a nex driver, half hour 'fore now.

RAS SIMI: Wha him name?

PASSION: One maager yout, drive a white Corolla.

RAS SIMI: Dat cyarn' help me.

PASSION: Me tink dem call im Cut up, true im hav nuff scar.

RAS SIMI: (*Kisses his teeth loudly.*) Chuh, me vex bout dat man. Sixty US garn.

PASSION: Wha mek? Yu never party las night?

RAS SIMI: Nah man. Me jus bun sum high grade an tink bout tings, til me drop a sleep. Yu party?

PASSION: Me and my inglis fren dance til we weak, mash up de whole place.

RAS SIMI: Nice man.

PASSION: (*Brightens.*) Yo, me love ah you know. When me yeye fall pon her in her bading suit, tings jus 'tan up stiff.

RAS SIMI: She can cook?

PASSION: (*Gives RAS a strange look.*) She nah haffi pick up a pot too quick.

RAS SIMI: She mus cook man.

PASSION: Watcha! We meet christmas jus pass, link up quarter dozen time and now she cum back to look fi mi. A good girl dat man. If she cyarn kneed dumplin nor fry fish me nah worry meself star. She soon learn.

RAS SIMI: Why yu tink she so quick fe reach back?

PASSION: How yu mean? She mus! Me give ah de best wuk. (*Laughs.*)

RAS SIMI: Me hear dem gyal deh like man fe eat (*With disgust.*) under sheet.

PASSION: (*Loudly.*) Yu mad? Yu know bad man nah bow. (*Two men touch fists.*) No nyam nyam, jus ram ram.

RAS SIMI: Innit bredrin. Sum of dese man yah tun sodomite fi get name bran shoe. Yu hav a good girl deh, she aks me fi carry him fren out lickle more.

PASSION: Him fren? Yu tink she rate you?

RAS SIMI: Him nah easy.

PASSION: Why you say dat?

RAS SIMI: She gwan like me do her sumting, she a fix herself so (*Folds arms and turns his back slightly from PASSION.*) and ben up her face so (*Pushes his lip out.*) 'fore me even talk to her.

PASSION: A lie. Dat nuh good.

RAS SIMI: She nah rate de rasta.

PASSION: Lissen dread, do like me, tink bout de red book and jus easy, seen.

RAS SIMI: Red book? Yuh too falla fashion, man. Dem tark bout de red book like it a bank book full a money.

PASSION: True dat. Wen me get tru and me soon get it boss. Mi pickney dem cyarn hungry again.

RAS SIMI: Me hear de same ting fram da one dem call Lucky. Idyat bwoy get sen fah 'fore dem mash up de runnins wid visa and wen him reach London him siddung an try live off ooman. She soon run him rars, nex ting him back on de beach a beg cigarette. Follow fool, yuh fool yuhself.

PASSION: A pussy 'ole dat. Yu si mi, mi nah fraid a wuk and me ready fi try a ting, wha eva it tek.

RAS SIMI: Clear conscience better dan big wage, mi sista learn dat de 'ard way.

PASSION: Me sorry fi ah but yuh tek yuh conscience to de store and si wha dem gi yuh.

RAS SIMI: Dat same tinking mek man value oil more dan life. Den all of yu wan run buil' up babylon fi dem to drop more bomb pon poor people and cripple African people dem wid debt. Yu nah member wha Garvey say?

PASSION: Yo, me jus wan feed mi pickney.

RAS SIMI: If yuh neva wear de boot, yuh wi neva feel de pinch. Yuh cyarn si sumting nuh right? Dem a foreign mek it so dat more while we eat dem food cah it cheaper, wear dem labels dat dem pay we fifteen dollars a *week* fi mek an check it, dem import everyting a yard fah free, free bumba claat trade dem call it, while man like we haffi pay tax on anyting we carry home. An dere yuh wan run too? Sumting nuh right.

PASSION: Sumting nuh right yes. (*Looks around before speaking in a hushed, vex voice.*) De bossman a bumba claat teef. Wuk mi wuk mi wuk and still me pocket dem

29

empty. Him tek one crate of Red Stripe fi pay we an den tek tree day fe count de money we mek fi him. Wha dat fah?

RAS SIMI: So it go my yout, dats why I and I do fi I and I. We haffi run tings bredrin nah let tings run we.

PASSION: Me hear Cyrus soon have him green card.

RAS SIMI: Green card, red book? All mi wan is a good black ooman.

PASSION: Look bout yuh Inglis fren.

RAS SIMI: She an African Queen, yuh nuh si it an she look like she need a fren.

PASSION: (*Suggestively.*) Dey all need a fren boss. Mek a move nuh?

RAS SIMI: Nah dem way deh.

PASSION: (*Kisses teeth.*) Si how man quick fi tek wha belong to yu becah yu too ley ley.

RAS SIMI: Wha fi yu cyarn be un fi yuh.

PASSION: (*Unconvinced.*) A so yu stay. Aright den, yu 'tan deh.

RAS SIMI: A so me stay.

Fade out.

Scene 3

BABS is sitting on a reclining beach chair, wearing a bikini and sunglasses. She is in her early thirties but looks ten years younger and feels it too. There is a beach towel on the chair, a bottle of lotion and the book, 'How Stella Got Her Groove Back' on her lap. She is looking out to sea and looks lost in a thought, which is filling her with happiness. She doesn't see or hear PASSION approach from behind until he is standing over her and speaks.

PASSION: W'happn sexy?

BABS: (*Smiling.*) Hi babe.

PASSION: Yuh look like yu a tink bout sumting good.

BABS: I am (*Self-consciously as he waits expectantly.*) I… I was just thinking how nice it will be…would be to never leave.

PASSION: Okay yuh avin a good day so far den?

BABS: It just got better.

PASSION: Dats nice man.

BABS: I met Cynthia earlier.

PASSION: Cyrus ooman?

BABS: Yeah, she's so funny. We ate at this little place up there pass Kuyaba, Chubby's I tink they call it…

PASSION: (*In recognition.*) Mmm.

BABS: …and she asked me, looking really worried (*In US accent.*) is it an indoor washroom or a galang? (*Laughs at memory.*)

PASSION: Wha dat?

BABS: Exactly. Apparently Cyrus took her to see his brother in the hills and when she wanted the toilet, he took her outside and went (*Points to the ground.*) galang.

PASSION: So dem live.

BABS: They're getting married yu know.

PASSION: Is it? (*Slight bitterness.*) Cyrus fine de rite one, dis one hav money. Me hear say she buy one big piece of lan.

BABS goes quiet and busies herself putting lotion on her arms and shoulders.

PASSION: Yuh wan mi fi do dat?

BABS: I'm almost done.

PASSION: Yu arite? (*Shouts across to someone passing.*)
    W'happen Short man?… (*Says with pride.*) Yeah man, my
    wife dis.

BABS: I'm fine.

PASSION: Me nah wan nutten fi wrong wid yu, yu no. If
    even maskitta bite yu me fret.

BABS: You get some new lyrics?

PASSION: Lyrics? No sah, why yu say dat?

BABS: So I'm your wife now, then.

PASSION: Jamaica tark dat. Me like yu dough, mi wan yu
    fah miself.

BABS: So what you going to do when you have me?

PASSION: How yu mean?

BABS: Well you have me… Cyrus is marrying Cynthia.

PASSION: Cyrus full a – (*Catches himself.*) Me nah watch
    man. Lissen baby, me love being around yu and me nah
    do nutten fi hurt yu feeling an I tink we could mek life
    yes.

BABS: Mmmm and?

PASSION: Me wish me had as much money fi tek care of
    yu so yu nah haffi pick up or put dun again. It hard a
    yard, yu si wha mi a say?

BABS: (*Brighter.*) I could get a job.

PASSION: Yasso, money nah run. Me hear in Inglan, pay
    betta.

SANDRA: (*Calling from a distance.*) Passion.

BABS: You're talking to the wrong person, I'm in debt up
to… (*She notices PASSION is distracted and looking behind
him.*) What is it?

PASSION: Oh shit.

BABS: What?

PASSION: (*Irritated.*) Soon come. (*Gets up.*)

> *SANDRA enters, in tight office wear and totally inappropriate
> shoes for the beach but instead of taking them off, she saunters
> over the sand, making an aggressive beeline for PASSION.
> He moves quickly to try and head her off but initially she is
> in earshot of BABS, mainly because her adopted middle class
> Jamaican accent is quite loud.*

SANDRA: (*Loudly, with the emphasis on the second syllable.*)
Passion!… Passion!

PASSION: (*Trying to manoeuver her away from BABS, he
speaks in an urgent whisper.*) Me busy right now.

SANDRA: Passion, me never get de money to send Susi
and Shanice to school.

PASSION: Me sen it man.

SANDRA: Passion, your ears hard? Me say me never get it.

PASSION: Wha you wan me fe do?

SANDRA: Be a man an sort it.

PASSION: Yuh bright gyal. Me say mi sen it wid your
nephew. Me nah hav it.

SANDRA: So how it vanish so?

PASSION: Teef mus a teef it man.

SANDRA: Teef? Bear excuse you have. You wan your children to get dere edication or yu wan dem fe en up like yu?

PASSION: (*Kisses his teeth then says in a hushed tone.*) Tap yuh noise man, me nah inna no passa passa today.

SANDRA: (*Loudly.*) You don't ave time for your children?

PASSION: Wha you a bait me for gyal? You can si me busy, man.

SANDRA: (*Still loud.*) Me can see dat yes. She hav any money?

PASSION edges SANDRA even further away from BABS and it's unclear to him whether she has overheard that.

PASSION: Why yu nah aks yuh new bwoy? Me 'ear him drive one big cyar.

SANDRA: Him hav him own mout dem to feed. You wan a nex man to raise your children?

PASSION: You shoulda tink bout dat before you tek your fars self to him bed.

SANDRA: No bodda speculate about my life. It none of your business.

PASSION: Yuh finish? (*Glances back at BABS who is getting ready to leave.*) Me hav me own business to tek care of.

SANDRA: She hav money? De black ones dem nah usually spen.

PASSION: Why yu so torment?

SANDRA: Susi and Shanice still haffi go to school, me need two nanny. (*Holds out her hand.*)

PASSION: (*Reluctantly.*) She nah hav no money.

SANDRA: (*In patois, clearly vex.*) You a lie down wid de rich tourist dem an still can't mek a raise? Yuh wutless!

PASSION: (*Kisses his teeth.*) Wha yuh tek me fah? Me nah stay like dat. Dis girl is cool man, big tings a gwan fe me. Nah try spwoil it.

BABS approaches and although PASSION's back is turned, SANDRA can see her coming.

SANDRA: So de gyal hav nuthin, no money and your pickney dem haffi go widout?

PASSION: Lissen, soon me can go an come a foreign regular and tek care of all of yu but right now…

BABS: (*Interrupts and speaks in a clipped voice, smiling.*) Is that right?

PASSION: (*Jumps.*) W'happn? Sorry me a tek time come.

PASSION tries to will SANDRA away with his eyes but she stays to enjoy his discomfort.

BABS: (*Raises her voice in patois.*) So which part a foreign you going?

PASSION begins to speak but BABS continues with a raised hand before he has a chance to speak.

In fact forget it, I heard enough. (*Turns to SANDRA.*) Sorry to interrupt. (*Begins to make a quick exit.*)

PASSION: Wait nuh!

PASSION starts to follow and BABS stops and turns.

Babs!

BABS: How many children you forget to tell me about?

PASSION: Lissen me can hexplain…

SANDRA: (*Shouts from a short distance, overlapping.*) Tree call him daddy, Shanice, Susi and Sean, six, five and two.

BABS: (*To herself.*) Rars.

PASSION: (*Overlapping.*) Gyal gimme two jacket fe wear.

SANDRA: (*Vex patois.*) Yu lickle rars yu, how yu can dash way yuh pickney so man? Dem might not tan hugly like yu but dem fava yuh bad still. Sean a dead stamp of yu. Face fava.

PASSION: Look, me hear say yu lose arf ah yu panty, so many man yu av.

SANDRA: Bumba claat. Yu still a believe dat shit. Lissen gyal, si dis man yah, him will service anyting, any make, mogel, age, condition, him nah disseminate, yu understan. One punni garn home, nudda one lan'. Member me tell yu so.

PASSION: Tu rars, a lie she a tell man. (*To SANDRA.*) A fuckry dat.

BABS: Well practice don't make perfect.

SANDRA: (*Screaming.*) Ahhhh, im nah 'tan lang pon de inglis gyal.

BABS exits. PASSION follows at a distant with SANDRA cussing as she exits.

(*Following PASSION.*) Where yu a go? Me nah finish wid yu yet, me wan me money seen, talking bout me under garment dem, yuh just vex cah yu cyan ave dis again, yu cyan mek me bawl out again, yu hear me Passion?… Passion?…

Scene 4

ANISHA is sitting at a cliffside bar preparing to watch the sunset. ANISHA has just turned thirty but looks in her early twenties. She is wearing white linen three quarter-length trousers and matching vest top with white slippers. She is looking out at the horizon with a look of complete contentment. Subconsciously, she is scratching her arm when RAS SIMI enters with a cocktail for her and a malt drink for himself.

RAS SIMI: De maskita a trouble you?

ANISHA: Believe. (*Scratches her leg.*) Thank you. (*She takes the drink and sips it straight away. She pulls a face not expecting it to be so strong.*)

RAS SIMI: No sah. (*He knocks away the scratching hand.*) I'll get you one lime. (*He picks a lime from a nearby tree and takes a ratchet knife out of his pocket to slice it in half.*) Rub it pon de bites.

ANISHA: Will it sting?

RAS SIMI: Maybe a bit but it will tap de itch.

ANISHA: (*Rubbing the lime on her arms and legs.*) Not drinking.

RAS SIMI: (*Shakes his head.*) Me nah really bodda wid dat, me a roots man. (*He looks out across the water.*) Sunset soon start.

ANISHA: The view from here is amazing.

RAS SIMI: (*Looking at her.*) Me see dat.

ANISHA: You're so lucky (*Sees he is looking at her and looks embarrassed.*)

RAS SIMI: Me lucky yes, me see dat too.

ANISHA looks uncomfortable and preoccupies herself with putting the lime on the bites on her arm.

ANISHA: I don't know what Babs told you, but I'm not really looking for… I don't want to seem ungrateful…

RAS SIMI: She tell me she hav da rite girl fi me.

ANISHA: Did she now?

RAS SIMI: Say she garn bring yu fram Inglan, come show me.

ANISHA: Is that right? Well, she didn't bring me anywhere. She came on one mission, I came on another and she doesn't know what that is… (*Sees he's smiling and stops.*) What?

RAS SIMI: Joke me a mek man.

ANISHA: Ha ha, very funny.

RAS SIMI: Me like ow yu look wen yu bex dough.

ANISHA: What did she really tell yu?

RAS SIMI: She aks me to take yu sumwhere nice and protect yu fram da gigolo dem.

ANISHA: (*Shaking her head.*) Like I can't take care of myself. (*Jokingly.*) Anyway, how do I know you're not one? Someone told me no true rasta would live here.

RAS SIMI: Who tell yu dat?

ANISHA: A true rasta. (*Smiles.*) Just someone I met.

RAS SIMI: Fus ting, me nah liv yah, me jus wuk.

ANISHA: Where do you live?

RAS SIMI: In da ills. Nex ting, ow yu no me nat a gigolo? Every fish inna de sea, nuh shark.

ANISHA: I was just joking.

RAS SIMI: A serious ting man. Camouflage dread a run up an dung wearin dem fashion locks fi get ooman but dem nah read a psalm yet or study heny of de teachins of Jah.

ANISHA: So you read the bible.

RAS SIMI: Yes man, me read Psalm 37 afta me lost me fare dis marning. Fret not dyself becah a evildoers, ah be (*Pauses.*) sumting bout de worker of iniquity rar rar rar and den me run me taxi til me ready fe link yu and mek back some of me money. So ow me no yu nat one a dem touris oo jus wan sample da big bamboo an den bruk a man art?

ANISHA: (*Smiling.*) That's exactly what I am.

RAS SIMI: Well mi art ready fi mash. Come nuh baby.

ANISHA: You really get women like that?

RAS SIMI: Yeah man, ow yu mean? Mi jus ear bout one fram Canada, one week she dideh and seven man she hav.

ANISHA: She's good man, I'd have taken Sunday off.

RAS SIMI: Yu a Christian?

ANISHA: Ish. I was raised an Aventist.

RAS SIMI: Yuh sabbat Sataday den?

ANISHA: I haven't practised for years. I still believe in God but I don't go to church anymore. I haven't been since I was a child.

RAS SIMI: White man use da church tu brainwash de African min'. Jamaica full a dem an look wha gwan.

ANISHA: You know a teacher once told me when the English came into Africa, they had the bible and we had the land. They said knee down and close your eyes and then they had the land, we had the bible.

RAS SIMI: Si it deh. Only Nigeria have more church dan yah and dem no betta off dan we. Wha Marley say now, (*Sings.*) emancipate yuhself fram mental slavery, none but ourself can free our min'.

ANISHA: That's my favourite song by Bob Marley, that one and Zimbabwe.

RAS SIMI: Yu know bout reggae music den?

ANISHA: I was born in England but that don't make me English.

RAS SIMI: Wha mek?

ANISHA: Is it your place of birth which defines you or your culture and your heritage? My parents were born here and I was raised (*Patois.*) wid ackee and sa'fish, rice and peas, soup pon Saturday, yam, green banana, cho cho, okra, snapper, mango, roast breadfruit, curry goat, reggae, lovers rock, rars and every udda claat known to man.

RAS SIMI: Bumba.

ANISHA: Dat one too. It didn't feel right when you called me a tourist earlier. I wasn't born here but I feel Jamaican.

RAS SIMI: How dat feel?

ANISHA: I feel like...like I've come home.

RAS SIMI: Member say yuh an African Queen. Africa is da true homeland of all black people.

ANISHA: I've never been to Africa so I don't know but this feels right to me. It's not a physical thing...it's kind of I...guess it's spiritual.

RAS SIMI: Welcome home den Empress.

ANISHA: (*Smiling.*) Thank you.

RAS SIMI: True dem say si mi and lib wid me a two different tings still.

ANISHA: It's all good so far.

RAS SIMI: Dat why yu come yah?

ANISHA: (*Surprised.*) Sorry?

RAS SIMI: Yu say yu neva tell yuh fren why yu come. Yu sound like yu a look fe sut'n, so yu fine it den?

Beat.

ANISHA: Not yet.

RAS SIMI: (*Joking.*) Well if it's a King yu wan, si mi yah.

ANISHA: (*Smiling.*) It's not that either. Thanks for the offer though.

RAS SIMI: No problem. Yuh a nice girl so fram me can 'elp, me deh ya.

ANISHA: (*Quietly.*) I appreciate that.

RAS SIMI: Which part yu famly fram? (*Dramatically distances himself.*) Nah tell me St Thomas?

ANISHA: (*Smiles.*) So dem say. Me nah wuk obeah pon yu dough.

RAS SIMI: Yo, two tings me nah fars inna, jugs an dat ting deh.

ANISHA: You don't smoke ganja then?

RAS SIMI: Ganja nah jug, it a 'erb, medicine. Wen me smoke it me deal inna iyah level a tinkin an meditation y'unerstan. It nuh tun man mad like dutty cocaine. Yu smoke it?

ANISHA: Once or twice back at University.

RAS SIMI: Me an yu haffi bun a spliff togedda. Yu still nah tell me weh yuh famly dem fram.

ANISHA: (*Reluctant.*) Hanover, I think.

RAS SIMI: Cooyah! My parish dat. Which part? Lucea, Green Islan, Orange Bay?

ANISHA: (*Uncomfortable.*) I'm not sure.

RAS SIMI: Wha yuh famly name?

ANISHA: (*Reluctantly.*) Brown.

RAS SIMI: Brown, Brown…bwoy me no sum people named so. Any of dem deh ya still?

ANISHA: (*Little distressed.*) Simi, I don't really wanna talk about it okay?

RAS SIMI stops and draws ANISHA's attention to the sunset.

RAS SIMI: A blessing dat. Look ow de sky come like a rainbow round de sun, me see aringe, yella, red, green.

ANISHA: Purple.

RAS SIMI: See it dere. Nutten cyan trouble yu man, God's dideh.

ANISHA: It's beautiful. I should have brought my camera.

RAS SIMI: Keep it yah (*Touches head.*) and deh ya. (*Touches chest near the heart.*)

They sit quietly watching the sunset in silence for a moment before ANISHA speaks quietly and slowly.

ANISHA: Simi, it's my dad, my dad's in Hanover.

Scene 5

BABS is sitting on her bed, there are photographs scattered and some are screwed up. She is on the phone and as she speaks she gets progressively agitated and angry.

BABS: Cynthia please… Cyn…ti…a (*In patois.*) yes, she in de apartment at de back… Me call earlier and I still can't remember de number…can someone go look please?… Yes I know you're busy but dis is urgent… Okay, tell her me call again. Thanks. (*Hangs up phone.*) For nothing.

RAS SIMI and ANISHA walk in.

RAS SIMI: Eveling.

ANISHA: Hiya.

BABS: Hi.

ANISHA: (*Looks at bed.*) Is everything alright?

BABS: Ask him.

ANISHA looks at RAS SIMI.

RAS SIMI: Me nuh no nutten, me jus a pass tru.

BABS: So yuh nuh no bout him ooman an tree pickney.

RAS SIMI: Him tell yu dat?

BABS: Dat rars? No, I got it first hand.

ANISHA: Oh shit man. You alright?

BABS: (*To RAS.*) You knew, didn't you?

RAS SIMI: Listen, me nah fars inna big man busness, me si an blin, ear and deaf.

BABS: Man tink dem can tek women fah idyat…

ANISHA: (*To RAS.*) I think you better go, I'll catch you later.

RAS SIMI: Yu say yu wan try Alfreds?

BABS: Don't let me spoil your fun.

RAS SIMI: Me sorry yu an Passion ketch up yeah.

BABS: Yu sorry him get ketch.

RAS SIMI: Lissen him arite, yu should tark to him.

BABS: Don't worry, me hav plenty fi say.

RAS SIMI: (*To BABS.*) Tek care of yuh friend. (*To ANISHA.*) Lickle more.

ANISHA: Thanks for today. See you later.

RAS SIMI exits.

BABS: (*Kisses her teeth.*) Blood claat.

ANISHA: Yo, it's not him you should be mad with. What happened?

BABS: I got played big style, that's what. You were right, they're all the damn same.

ANISHA: I never said that.

BABS: Da rasta sweet you so yuh change your tune now?

ANISHA: I don't remember saying it. What happened?

BABS: The usual. Meet man, like man, listen to man's shit, man lies, ting dies and dat's the end of it. What's happening with you?

ANISHA: Forget me. Are you okay?

BABS: I'm cool. Come on, I want all the gossip.

ANISHA: Well, you were right.

BABS: What, they're all the same?

ANISHA: No, when you said I would like him.

BABS: I'm hardly a reliable judge of character but go on.

ANISHA: (*Coyly.*) I don't know… He seems nice, really nice.

BABS: (*Aside.*) Don't they always? And? What did you do?

ANISHA: Not what you might think. We went up to Ricks, it was amazing, really beautiful.

BABS: You're going to see him again then?

ANISHA: Later, I think at the beach party (*Hesitates.*) if you wanna go

BABS pulls a face.

if not we're meeting up tomorrow anyway.

BABS: (*Trying to sound enthusiastic.*) Going anywhere nice?

Beat.

ANISHA: (*Cautiously.*) I'm going to see my father.

BABS: (*Taken aback.*) Where's he buried?

ANISHA: He's not.

BABS: Cremated?

ANISHA shakes her head, smiling wryly.

ANISHA: You think I'm going to look at a pile of ashes?

BABS: (*Perplexed.*) I thought he was dead.

ANISHA: I only wished he was.

They are both silent. BABS doesn't quite know how to react. She searches ANISHA's face to see if she is joking but only sees pain there.

BABS: (*Lightly.*) Remind me not to get on your bad side.

ANISHA: (*Smiling.*) It's a bit late for that.

BABS: He must have done something really bad.

ANISHA: Mmmm.

BABS: Do you wanna talk about it?

ANISHA doesn't speak for a while but looks sad and uncomfortable.

ANISHA: I'm building this up and it's silly really… (*Takes a deep breath.*) I was nine when he left, there I've said it, three days before my tenth birthday.

BABS: (*Gently.*) Go on.

ANISHA: I was a real daddy's girl and it was only because of him that I actually felt like I belonged in our family. You know I've never got on with my mum.

BABS: I know.

ANISHA: Well it got worse after he went. I caught him sneaking out early one morning and I said daddy where you going, because I thought maybe I could go too and he said he was going to buy my birthday present and not to tell anyone. It was going to be a big surprise. He had this huge bag, I don't know why I didn't ask him about it but I thought, maybe he was going to America to get my roller skates or something. How stupid is that?

BABS: You were a child, why wouldn't you think that?

ANISHA: I waited all day for him, I wouldn't even blow my candles out because I wanted to hold on until he came. Eventually Anthony said, hurry up and make your wish, wish the old man comes back if you have to, I want some cake.

BABS: Brothers, so bloody sensitive.

ANISHA: He hasn't changed has he? Anyway I made my wish, cut the cake, posed for some photographs and played with the stupid Rubik's cube Clive got for me.

BABS: What did you wish for?

ANISHA: I wished he was dead. If you see the pictures, I look like a normal ten year but inside, off camera, I was angry, heartbroken and ashamed all in one. I know it sounds crazy but it was easier to think he was dead than believe he had lied to me and left me without even saying goodbye. It was easier to deal with that than to accept he didn't love me.

BABS: Of course he loved you.

ANISHA: (*Sharply.*) How do you know? Is that what you do to someone you love?

BABS: I can't speak for him but maybe he had no choice. Did you ever find out why he left?

ANISHA: Not really. I heard rumours, like he returned to some dark skinned woman back home, his childhood sweetheart or something and he'd only sent for mum because she was brown and she had better chances. Shit like that. Can you believe that slave mentality?

BABS: I can believe it, it still goes on but it was worse back then.

ANISHA: About five months ago my Aunt phoned out of the blue to say he was ill and could we send some money for treatment. It was his kidneys, I think. That was the first I knew he was still alive.

BABS: What did you do?

ANISHA: Nothing. I thought about it, I mean I didn't want him on my conscience but Anthony and Clive said they'd cover it so I left them to it. I'm glad really. (*Bitterly.*) Can you believe he had mum's number all those years and couldn't even be bothered to call?

BABS: I had no idea. I'm so sorry, I've been so caught up in my own crap and… (*Shakes her head.*) if there's anything I can do, just let me know.

ANISHA: Simi is going to help me find him. He's been really cool, you know. Anyway, he knows Hanover quite well because of his taxi work so we'll see. I don't have much to go on, I know he's a Pastor now but that's all.

BABS: Why don't you call Anthony and see what he knows. He must have a contact for your Aunt.

ANISHA: That's true. I know it might be a wild goose chase but I have to try.

BABS: You've got to do what you think's best. If I was in your shoes, I'd probably do the same. What are you going to say when you find him?

ANISHA: (*Pauses then says in patois.*) Ah yu me fadda? Where's my rars claat present?

Scene 6

Light dims, dancehall music starts to play, some tracks on the latest rhythm and slowly the lights come up, same scene but time has lapsed. BABS is standing over ANISHA tonging her hair. ANISHA is dressed to party and BABS is still in her underwear and she is dancing to the music while she works.

ANISHA: You have to teach me the new moves before we go.

BABS: I haven't caught it myself yet, Passi…that rars tried to teach me last night. It's goes something like… (*She plays 'Elephant Man 'Pon De River, Pon De Bank' and does a quick demonstration that ANISHA tries to follow.*)

ANISHA: (*Giving up.*) I'm hardly gonna set the place alight. Are you sure you wanna go?

BABS: I'm cool, if I see him, I'll go about my business same way. Are you sure you wanna go?

ANISHA: I feel better already, It looks like Anthony might come through.

BABS: I hope so, for your sake.

ANISHA: He's sure they've got an address, he's belling me later. He's a bit worried about me doing it on my own.

BABS: I'm worried about you too. Don't get your hopes up too high.

ANISHA: I'm more concerned about you tonight. I know how you can stay with your hot head and if you see Passion, which chances are you will…

BABS: (*Forcefully.*) I'm cool, okay.

ANISHA: O…kay.

BABS: Okay, maybe I'm still a bit vex but that girl, his baby mother, made it sound like all I meant to him was between my two foot. I felt cheap. It wouldn't be so bad but it's not like he's all that, in that department, anyway.

ANISHA: I thought you said…

BABS: Yeah yeah, he was alright once or twice but I'm certain that was luck more than judgement…

Door knocks.

…if that's him.

ANISHA: Do you want me to let him in?

BABS: (*Holding the tongs in a threatening way.*) And lock the door behind him.

ANISHA: You're cool remember. Put something on.

As BABS steps into her dress and pulls it on, ANISHA goes to open the door.

PASSION stands there looking sheepish, BABS picks the tongs back up.

PASSION: What's up? Babs deh deh?

ANISHA lets him in and BABS gets up like she's going to fly at him. ANISHA unwittingly finds herself standing between them.

BABS: Wha de fuck yu want?

PASSION: Nah bodda cuss bad word to big man seen, it nah fit yuh.

BABS: Wha de rars dat gotta do wid yu? I was just telling Nish shit yu a deal wid in bed, considering you get so much practice.

PASSION: Who yu a tark too so gyal?

BABS: You. You deaf? All you do is spread my legs far as you can an jook like your life depen pon it.

PASSION: So wen yu a call out, yu nah enjoy it den?

ANISHA: I'm going. (*ANISHA takes the tongs out of BABS' hand and tries to finish her hair.*)

BABS: Who do ya tink you are anyway, playing all these women off, when you don't have shit to offer 'em?

PASSION: Who are dese ooman? You a lissen to dat mad gyal? Yu nah si she bex cah a wha me say to ah?

BABS: Who wouldn't be vex wid a wutless baby fadda like yu?

ANISHA: I'm think I should leave you two to…talk.

PASSION: Whey yu no no bout, no chat bout. De gyal too lie. She spen off de money pon foolishness den cum hype up himself an mek noise ina me 'ead wen it run out.

ANISHA: Later.

BABS: Wait nuh. (*To PASSION.*) It's you dats too lie. How come you neva told me you had children?

PASSION: Yu neva aks. Me nah lie bout dem but we nah tark bout weda we breed? Yuh might hav pickney too but we nah mad bout it. A fi yu busness dat.

ANISHA runs a comb through her hair and then exits discreetly while they are talking.

BABS: You knew I didn't have children.

PASSION: All me know is me rate you bad, bad, bad baby…

BABS: Well I hate you.

PASSION: Me nah wan us fi mash up ova dis.

BABS: Too late.

PASSION: Wha me do yu man? Me nah do nutten fi hurt yuh feelings.

BABS: You've lied and you've cheated.

PASSION: Me tell yu aready me neva lie. An cheat? Me hav fren dats all, nutten like wha me an yu have. (*PASSION's phone rings and he barely looks down at it before cutting it off.*) Chuh, yu haffi unerstan, me wages dem lickle bit man so me haffi try a ting sumtime fi mek a raise. Yu si me?

BABS: So you're a gigolo?

PASSION: Nah man, yu bright. Gigolo run back a ooman, white, him want it, black, him want it, fat, him want it, ol', he want it, hugly, him want it. Me hav fren but me nah lie down wid dem. Jus fren, dats hall.

BABS: So how come you have all these labels like Nike and D'n'G if you nah have money?

PASSION: Nah mi money tek buy dem. Sumtime if mi fren dem rate me, dem carry sumting fi me nex time dem come. Dats all. Same like yu did. Me love dem shirt yu bring baby.

BABS: That makes me feel much betta.

PASSION: Me neva wen tu 'igh school yu no. Deres seven ah we in da fambly an dem neva hav it fe sen me, tru me Black… De brudda wha falla me, Brown, dem call him, dem spen dem lars fi gi him a start in life, tinking him go mek doctor or sumting. On a marnin me wud rake de yard an fetch wata fram de standpipe while him a fix up himself inna shirt an tie wid him bag on him back, fulla books. Sumtime me jus feel fe dash rockstone afta him an lick him in him neckback. It's 'ard fi get tru wid no subjects an ting. But me wan mi pickney dem tu go tu clars, straight tru. Dem alone we wuk fah. Dats de only reason me wan go a foreign, so mi can tek care of dem rite, y'unerstan?

BABS: I understand but…

PASSION: (*Cuts in, in a charming voice.*) De udda reason is, of course…

BABS: (*Interrupts.*) Your brother, did he become a doctor?

PASSION: Him a doctor ahrite, a rars weed doctor. Him nuh like 'ard work, him hav it too easy.

BABS: Anyway, I hope you're not suggesting coming to England with me because you don't have a hope.

PASSION: Bwoy, yuh look sexy wen yuh bex dough.

BABS: Piss off.

PASSION: (*Joking.*) Look ow yu get serious pon me tu backfoot. Yu a bad me up terrible. Me fraid fi come tru de door, tink yu garn lick me. And yu cyarn tek lick.

BABS smiles despite herself.

(*Picks up screwed up picture off the bed.*) Dis yu wan do me? (*Straightens out picture.*) Fadda, me look boasie no rars. Dats de nite me met, don't it?

BABS: (*Surprised.*) You remember?

PASSION: How yu mean? (*Animated.*) Me member me nat lang finis wuk and me hat bad man an yu and yuh fren pars by lookin sumwhere fi nyam sum good food. Me offer tu show yu one place up de beach but me haffi bade fus so yu buy two drink, cocktails me tink and wait fi me. While me a soap up, yu deh pon me min' de whole time, me tink ow dat lickle pink dress yu hav on fit yu gud. Lawd mek me rinse off fars.

BABS: (*Laughs.*) You were kinda quick.

PASSION: Me still smell good dough, me wear one spray fram de US an me feel criss. Me feel a way bad wen yu aks me to join yu an me neva hav as much money fi eat but yu buy sum mannish wata and fry chicken fi me and me tink, a nice girl dis man.

BABS: So that's why you like me?

PASSION: Nah man.

BABS: So wha?

PASSION: Me tell yu aready yu is a good girl…an me like ow de pum pum fat. (*Laughs.*)

BABS: A wha dis?

PASSION: A good sut'm dat man.

BABS: (*Smiles.*) In that case thanks… I think…

The hotel room phone rings.

Saved by the bell, I'm going to take it. (*Answers phone.*) Hello…yes, that's me… (*Shocked.*) What? (*Worried.*) what happened?… Okay Sav-La Mar, I'm coming now… Thanks.

PASSION: W'happn?

BABS: (*Putting on her shoes as she speaks.*) It's Cynthia. She's in hospital.

Scene 7

ANISHA and RAS SIMI are sitting at a table at the beach party. ANISHA is eating a fried chicken dinner and has a cocktail and RAS SIMI is drinking a malta. Reggae music is playing and out of their view, one woman is wining to the music, dancing provocatively in a tight-fitting outfit. She is dancing to wine like a gypsy – Elephant Man.

ANISHA: If Passion don't come soon bwoy…

RAS SIMI: Soun like him either dead or dem garn a bed. Me sorry fi him.

ANISHA: (*Shrugs.*) Me sorry fi her… You sure you don't wanna try some?

RAS SIMI: Strictly ital food me eat, me haffi cook fi yu one time.

ANISHA: That would be nice. I hope Babs manages to hold it down. Come like she was going to bun him with the curling tongs before I left.

RAS SIMI: (*Laughing.*) You Inglis girls nah easy man.

ANISHA: Dats cause we were only born in England, come like an accident of birth. I'm sure the way we stay fiery so, we mus hav maroon blood run tru we veins.

RAS SIMI: Lissen, yu kno say dem sen hall de renkest, most feisty slaves dem yasso. De ones dat gi bear trouble pon de ship an everyting, de warriors dem. No udda islan wud tek dem, so Jamaica dem come. Dats ow we en up wid de wickedest rebellion and ow sum of we still renk no rars. Yo, if a maroon yu a descend fram, me nah fars wid yu, no t'all.

ANISHA: (*Smiling.*) I feel say Nanny of the Maroons, fi mi Nanny dat. I'll have to ask my father when I see him. (*Agitated, takes out phone and checks it.*) Why hasn't Anthony called back?

RAS SIMI: (*Checks watch.*) A middle marning in Cup a tea Country, don't it?

ANISHA: He said he'd call back tonight. (*Pause.*) How do you know that?

RAS SIMI: (*Cautiously.*) Me hav people in Inglan.

Enter SANDRA at a distance. RAS sees her before she sees him.

Bwoy trouble a come.

ANISHA: Who's that?

RAS SIMI: Your fren henemy. Chuh, cockroach hav no busness ah fowl dance.

SANDRA approaches.

SANDRA: (*With distaste.*) What's gwarning rasta?

RAS SIMI: Me deh ya. Yu tun party girl?

SANDRA: Like yu, me a try a ting. Where's yuh wukless fren?

RAS SIMI: Me nuh no henyone named so.

SANDRA: (*Looking around.*) Him nuh deh ya? Me come fe get what's mines.

RAS SIMI: Wha yu fi get, yuh fi get wen yu fi get it.

SANDRA: (*Distracted by something she's seen.*) Watcha! Gyal part out a door an she jus breed da udda day…him mus wan me fi tun whore like she.

RAS SIMI: Him tek care ah tings.

SANDRA: Looks so, on de beach all day a look ooman.

RAS SIMI: So him jus fi wuk? Him wuk double lars week.

SANDRA: Den him should mek double money an me cyarn get single. Why yu a tek up fi him? It nuh jus me dat suffah, it's da children dem.

RAS SIMI: Ow much yuh need?

SANDRA: (*After consideration.*) Tree nanny.

RAS SIMI: Me hav five bills. Dat mus cover yu til wen. (*Pushes notes into her hand.*) Mek sure yuh man nah tek it fram yu.

SANDRA: (*Disgusted.*) A teef wouldn't wan. Wha dis garn buy? (*Puts note in her bra.*)

RAS SIMI: Dem edication. Yu tink me nuh no bout school fees?

SANDRA: True yu a look bout yuh sista pickney dem but if certain man an man had taken care of business, she would neva fly a foreign an get lock up in da fus place.

RAS SIMI: (*Cuts in.*) Go look bout yuh pickney. Dem hav school a marning.

SANDRA: (*Kisses teeth again.*) An while de muddas tek care of de pickney, where de faddas dem? A gi de zoom zoom to every foreign pum pum dem can fine. It nah matter wha wrong wid yu, deres a man deh ya in Jamaica fe yu. Look at she, so big, she look like she nyam out de whole supermarket one time. She nah see her pum pum for ten years but him manage fe fine it. Him go down dere and eat as much pork for as much money and den wake up an call himself rasta. (*As she says rasta with real emphasis, she looks directly in RAS SIMI's eye. Kisses her teeth again.*) Me garn.

SANDRA exits.

ANISHA: Bwoy.

RAS SIMI: Well a gud ting me gi ah me lars money or she might ah get really renk.

ANISHA: (*Cautiously.*) What she was saying about your sister…is it true?

RAS SIMI: Bwoy, me nuh really know wha fi tell yu, one day she a sell ackee pon de roadside an nex she a call fram foreign jail…me still cyarn believe wha gwarn, me nah tell yu no lie. Dem time deh, she a beg money marning, noon an evelin but me neva pay ah no mine cah true she ofen tek money fram me to try keep up wid one hottie hot gyal Delsina, who always a flex in da latest sinting an me cyarn support dat again. Same time me cyar nah run so good so me haffi spen a wholeheap to get it back on da road straight, so me can run taxi. Nex ting, she tell me mudda she a go town to look bout sum papers an to mine her pickney dem till she come. All now, she cyarn reach back

ANISHA: (*Quietly.*) Was it drugs?

RAS SIMI: True Delsina get tru an mek bout J$100,000, so she tink she mus get tru. Me mudda say (*In accent.*) wen her belly hungry she fill it wid cocaine an nah cum to yu, an idyat ting dat. Me feel a way bad, me cyarn even tell her how it go. I sen her pickney dem to school cah edication is de key to liberation. Me nah wan dis fi happen again.

ANISHA: When can she come home?

RAS SIMI: Bwoy, de nex tree, four years. It rough man, but so it go still.

ANISHA: I'm really sorry. You must wanna see her bad?

RAS SIMI: How yu mean? She say de food alone ah kill ah. She tell me bout one toad in da 'ole sitin, all now me nuh no a wha. (*ANISHA is poised to speak.*) An me nuh wan no. I would visit her yes but tru da (*Sarcastic.*) mudda country wan blame man a yard fi all dem problems, dem a keep we out wid visa.

ANISHA: They've made it harder but it's not impossible, they say they're trying to cut down on guns and (*Pauses.*) drugs crime.

RAS SIMI: Yu see heny factory a mek guns a yard? Yu see anyting grow yah cept ganja? Chuh dis ting is bigger than dis lickle island yah man and visa nah do nutten cept keep da economy down an starve Air Jamaica an tap mudda fram see daughter, brudda fram see sista...

ANISHA's mobile phone rings and she answers it with a sense of urgency.

ANISHA: Hello... (*Louder.*) Hello...wait I can't hear you very well. (*To RAS.*) Sorry, I'll soon come back.

ANISHA exits. RAS SIMI watches her go, then casually sits back and takes a drink. PASSION approaches him from behind.

PASSION: (*Looking at the plate.*) Ow's da fowl Ras?

RAS SIMI: It nah fi mi. (*They touch fists.*) She nah kill yu den?

PASSION: A she garn a 'ospital.

RAS SIMI: Yu neva...?

PASSION: Could neva. She arite man, a Cyntia she falla deh.

RAS SIMI: Wha Cyrus do now?

ANISHA has found a quieter spot and the audience can now hear her conversation. PASSION and RAS remain on stage in unheard conversation.

ANISHA: He did what? Say that again… Am I sitting? No, just tell me… I said just tell me…

As ANISHA takes in the contents of the phonecall, occasionally she nods her head and she begins to look visibly shocked. She leans on a wall or a chair for support.

(*In a small, shaky voice.*) Yeah, I'm still here… (*Quietly.*) I can't believe it.

ANISHA's legs begin to give way and she lowers herself into a semi-crouching position and places her head in one hand. At this point we return to the conversation with PASSION and RAS SIMI.

RAS SIMI: Me cyarn believe. So it go for real?

PASSION: Umm huh, pure distress im a bring ooman.

RAS SIMI: Me sorry fi ah man. (*RAS SIMI starts looking in the direction ANISHA walked in.*) Me soon come.

PASSION: (*Laughing.*) Yu tun watch man now?

RAS SIMI: Me care bout dis girl an me jus feel a vibe still…

PASSION: Wha, dun so? (*Beckons to RAS SIMI's nether regions.*)

RAS SIMI: Me say me soon come.

RAS SIMI finds ANISHA who is still visibly upset and draws her to her feet.

RAS SIMI: (*Concerned.*) W'happen to yu?

ANISHA: That was Anthony.

Scene 8

Bedroom scene. The room is in semi-darkness as the curtains are still drawn and ANISHA's bed is occupied while BABS' is untouched. ANISHA is on the side of the bed nearest the audience. The fan is on and is directed at ANISHA's bed only. The door opens slowly and BABS creeps in, tiptoes to her bed, only glancing at ANISHA to check she has not disturbed her. She bends down and uses a lighter to look in her case and pulls out a bathing suit.

ANISHA: (*Low voice.*) It's okay, it'll be fine.

BABS: (*Whispers.*) Nish, you're dreaming again. (*Pause.*) Anisha.

ANISHA: Good morning…it is morning isn't it? (*Sits up.*) How's Cynthia?

BABS: You heard then? She's okay, all things considered. Did Passion tell you what happened?

ANISHA: Uh huh. What was she drinking?

BABS: White rum, at least half a bottle. That fucking Cyrus has a lot to answer for but you can't trust any of them. None of them have your back but all of them want your front! I tell you, I know Ras might seem nice but just be careful okay…

ANISHA: (*Overlapping.*) Babs…

RAS SIMI: Good marning.

BABS: Bumba. Er good morning. (*To ANISHA.*) Don't tell me, it's not what I think.

ANISHA: It's not.

BABS: Rars, well I stand by what I say. (*Short laugh.*) To rahtid, me cyarn believe…

RAS SIMI sits at the side of the bed. He is wearing boxer shorts and quickly gets dressed.

ANISHA: You don't have to go.

BABS: No, stay. Please. I was going for a swim anyway.

RAS SIMI: Me soon come back. Me ah go bade fus an put gas in de tank. Lickle more.

BABS: Not even a kiss she get?

Self-consciously, RAS kisses ANISHA on the forehead before he exits.

ANISHA: Before you even start…

BABS: What? (*Laughing.*) Me nah say nutten. You're a big woman and he's a big man…is he a big man…? (*Laughs harder.*)

ANISHA: (*Indignant.*) I wouldn't know.

BABS: It's alright, you don't have to tell me.

ANISHA: I won't. I'm glad Cynthia's okay. I tried calling the hospital last night but because I didn't know her last name…

BABS: The people from her apartment called me. They found her being really sick. I was glad Passion was here but when I found out what happened, I was so angry. It made me realise that I didn't love him because I would never do that over him, no matter what.

ANISHA: Do what, get drunk? You do that all the time.

BABS: She took tablets too. Because the drink made her so sick, they didn't have a chance to get into her system. She was lucky.

ANISHA: Not that lucky.

BABS: Can you imagine? She's sitting at the front of this taxi an two man are at the back talking about Cyrus' woman, how she is in Jamaica, they're getting married and how he made her one ring. Cynthia's feeling quite good at this point. Next thing they're saying she's from Toronto…

ANISHA: And she's from DC.

BABS: And even worse, they know where she's staying which is about a mile and a half from Cynthia's place. She had to stop the car because she thought she was going to throw up.

ANISHA: Passion said she went to confront her.

BABS: She only tried to find her to see if it was true but she'd gone out for the day with some man…

ANISHA: Cyrus by any chance?

BABS: Oh no, he was in the hills all day farming.

ANISHA: Yeah right, well you reap what you sow.

BABS: Well you should know, Ras ah sow his wil' oats dem. I leave you alone for five minutes…

ANISHA: Like I said nothing happened. (*Smiling.*) But I do like him. We're going to look for my dad today. Listen, Anthony came through. He didn't have an address but we know which area.

BABS: Nice one. I'm happy for you.

ANISHA: That's not all, get this. Mum came clean. Apparently for about two years dad wrote letters and sent cards but she kept them from us, to protect us apparently. She hoped we would just forget him. I think he must have stopped when he never got any reply. And, he did send me a present for my birthday. The skates mum gave me the following christmas were from him. Anthony was so excited when he told me, like he was shedding a massive weight but he was worried about me too. All them years they thought I didn't care, especially when we heard he was sick. I was in shock, it just hit me and next minute, I'm bawling like a baby. That's why Simi stayed. He didn't want to leave me alone.

BABS: How do you feel now?

ANISHA: I don't even know, mixed really, I guess. I've missed out on a relationship with him for over twenty years. Twenty years. (*Shakes her head.*) I feel angry with mum in one way but Simi was saying she probably did what she thought was right at the time. It wasn't out of spite.

BABS: He left her too.

ANISHA: I know, I know and she didn't fall apart. I'm going to call her later, I feel I need too talk to her.

BABS: I'm glad. I hope you find him but try and prepare yourself, just in case.

ANISHA: Anthony and Simi said the same thing. Some of my questions have been answered but do you know what I really want to know? Is he proud of me? Will he approve of the way I've lived my life.

BABS: How can you doubt it? Doing accountancy is big tings no matter how you look it.

ANISHA: I'm not there yet. Feels like I've got a zillion exams to pass.

BABS: You make a success of everything you put your mind too. You don't procrastinate your way through life like I do. Anyway, your father's a pastor so he'll be more interested in your qualities, your virtues… (*Looks concerned.*)

ANISHA: What is it?

BABS: You're a heathen so you only have (*Glances at her watch.*) a few hours to turn it around.

ANISHA: (*Laughing.*) Thanks friend.

BABS: If he had a daughter like me, then he'd be worried.

ANISHA: Why do you say that?

BABS: I've just drifted through life, being indecisive, never having a real career like you, just moving from job to job.

ANISHA: I think you're being too hard on yourself. We're not all supposed to be the same, that's what makes the World as fascinating as it is.

BABS: What's fascinating about people judging you on how different you are, judging you on what you have or don't have, on how you look, how you could loss a few pounds or gain a few. People spend so much time watching everyone else, they forget to look in the mirror. Nothing works for me back home, it feels like the big hand on the clock no longer moves. I'm just stagnating. I want to live my life, really live, not be a observer.

ANISHA: If you don't like something, then change it. To thine own self be true, that's what my mother used to say.

BABS: That's exactly what I intend to do. I'm not going home. I've made my list of pros and cons and there was only one con.

ANISHA: Money, right.

BABS: Exactly.

ANISHA: Which is a pretty big con.

BABS: Well I'm tired of measuring my life in material terms. All the money I make I use to escape anyway. The emptiness I feel inside can't be filled by cash. It's a spiritual hunger I need to feed.

ANISHA: Not to mention a sexual one.

BABS: I'm being serious.

ANISHA: So am I. If you've met a man who makes you happy you shouldn't let him get away so easily. True happiness is so rare.

BABS: This isn't about him, it's about me. Being here and soaking up the magic, I just want to be able to sustain that the best I can. Passion doesn't really come into the equation. We're cut from the same cloth. He was looking to me for a way out and I was looking to him, so we do have something in common. Or at least we did.

ANISHA: You're really not going back?

BABS: No. I left my heart here the last time I came and I thought it was with him. I was trying to make him fit, the way Cynthi and that Cyrus the virus fit together. I admired her because she was brave enough to give up everything and take a chance on love but look how that turned out.

ANISHA: It doesn't mean the same will happen to you and Passion.

BABS: There is no me and Passion. Anyway, Cynthia has already decided she's going to stay on here, despite what's happened and she said I can share her apartment until I sort myself out.

ANISHA: I don't think you should write him off though.

BABS: Let it go. I've made up my mind, I'm moving on.

ANISHA: To what though?

BABS: Put it this way, he's not the only egg in my basket.

ANISHA: At least you have a basket.

BABS: Cynthia's doctor asked for my number last night.

ANISHA: How romantic. Was that before or after he pumped her stomach?

BABS: She was fine by then. He was quite nice actually and I don't see anything wrong with having a back-up plan.

ANISHA: (*Unconvinced.*) Whatever you say. Will you come with us today, to look for my father?

BABS: Of course, definitely. I just need to go for a swim first. Imagine, I'll be able to do that every morning from now on.

ANISHA: I'm already tempted to join you, so don't. (*Pause.*) One more thing about today.

BABS: Mmmm, go on.

ANISHA: Passion will be coming too.

Scene 9

RAS SIMI, PASSION, ANISHA and BABS are sitting in RAS' stationary car, parked on a hill in the middle of Country. RAS and ANISHA are sitting at the front and the other two are at the back. BABS' body is turned away from PASSION and she is trying to put distance between them without much success. They all look a bit hot, bothered and fed up.

RAS SIMI: Me feel say it dideh. (*Beckons up with head.*)

BABS: Yu feel say? When you know say, den tell me.

PASSION: Yu should ah bear lef, dun so.

RAS SIMI: Bear pot 'ole me did ah see, we couldn't parce.

BABS: Yu would a drive down one gully, listening to him.

PASSION: Wha yu no bout gully?

BABS: I know if you don't move from me, that's where your mudda garn fine yu.

PASSION: 'Ear dis gyal yah. Yu nuh no me.

BABS: Yu a threaten me now?

RAS SIMI: Mout him a mout yu.

ANISHA: Why don't you two jus kiss and make up? (*To RAS.*) Shall we go?

RAS SIMI: Come nuh.

BABS: Go where? All me see is pure bush.

ANISHA: We can find someone to ask.

PASSION: Me tell yu aready, a wrong move we mek.

BABS: That's nothing new for you.

RAS SIMI: Cool nuh man, mek me get mi bearings.

BABS: When have I heard that before? Was it the first or second time we stopped?

RAS SIMI: T'ird time lucky.

ANISHA: (*To BABS.*) You're not helping. Go look for someone to ask.

BABS: Me nah tark to duppy an we left the living lang time.

PASSION: Wha kin a argument dat? People live yah. Look up so (*Pointing.*) right up dere tru de trees. Yu nah see 'ouse?

BABS and ANISHA follow his hand.

ANISHA: That's miles away.

BABS: Me look like bird?

RAS SIMI: (*Smiling.*) Dis gyal nah easy at all. Lissen, me tink deres one store and ting bout five minutes fram yah.

BABS: There you go, thinking again. If it's all the same to you, I'll sit this one out. (*Starts scratching her leg.*)

PASSION: (*To RAS.*) Yu hav yuh cutlass, my yout?

RAS SIMI: Me lef it yu no bredrin. Me jus hav one blade.

PASSION: Yu know, me look pon me mashait 'fore me come out but me feel say yu would have it.

BABS: (*Aside.*) A poppy show dis. (*Still scratching her legs.*)

RAS SIMI: Chuh, we'll try a ting still. Me grow a bush so… (*To ANISHA.*) Yu ready?

ANISHA: Let's go.

RAS SIMI gets out the car and goes round to ANISHA's side.

PASSION: (*To BABS.*) Maskitta hat yu? Nah cratch dem. (*To RAS SIMI through window.*) Ras, see if you can fine sut'm fi ah.

ANISHA: (*Getting out the car.*) Who tell her fi wear shorts, come a Country?

BABS: I was hot.

PASSION: (*Smiling.*) Yu hav good legs man, yu skin clean an pretty? Tap cratching.

BABS: Whatever.

ANISHA: Are there any lime trees here?

PASSION: Lawd yu tun bush gyal now?

RAS SIMI: Me nah see none. Let's wark lickle bit an see.

PASSION: Yu hav signal pon yuh phone?

RAS SIMI: (*Pulls phone from his pocket.*) Jus one bar me hav.

ANISHA: Same here.

PASSION: If anyting call, yeah an we'll buck up on yu.

BABS: Yu one.

PASSION: Me cyarn leave yu. It soon dark.

BABS: I hav a lighter.

RAS SIMI: She nuh no dark yet.

ANISHA: Come on let's go.

RAS SIMI: Soon come.

BABS: Nish?

ANISHA: Mmm.

BABS: If yu reach a store, get me one bottle of water.

PASSION: Water done?

ANISHA: Yu alone drink tree bottles.

BABS: Tell him again.

RAS SIMI: Yu cyarn buy wata yah. No touris dideh.

BABS: Dem hav sense.

PASSION: Yu forget why you come?

ANISHA: Thank you.

BABS: Sorry Nish. Just buy me anyting okay. As long as it's wet. Good luck.

ANISHA: Later.

> *RAS SIMI and ANISHA start to walk away and RAS takes ANISHA's arm.*

RAS SIMI: Me nah wan yu fi lick yu 'ead pon rockstone.

ANISHA: Thanks.

PASSION: Why yu so miserable?

BABS: I didn't ask you to stay.

PASSION: Me love yu still, dough.

BABS: Please.

PASSION: Lissen, me nah sleep las nite, a tink bout yu.

BABS: Here we go. (*Calls to ANISHA and RAS.*) Yo, wait up. I'm coming.

PASSION: (*Calls.*) She nah go nowhere. (*To BABS.*) A serious ting man. Ow you feisty an dat, me no say yu true feelins yu wan hide baby.

BABS: No, you ah get me real feelings.

PASSION: (*Looks her straight in her eye. She won't hold his gaze.*) Look pon me nuh. Me say me love you.

BABS: (*Makes a move to get out the car.*) I need some air. Don't dis bwoy believe in AC.

PASSION: Da cyar nah run.

BABS: Well, when it did, I was still frying.

PASSION: Yu love moan e. (*Takes his bandana from his pocket and starts to fan her with it.*) Dat better?

BABS: Little bit…thanks.

After a moment she stops his hand.

Look, it won't work.

PASSION: Me can do it fars.

BABS: Don't I know this… I'm sorry, I meant me and you, we won't work.

PASSION: Why nat? (*PASSION's phone rings and he cuts it off without checking it, shaking his head.*) Dem nah call yet. Why yu say dat?

BABS: You want to come to England, right?

PASSION: Jus fi mek sum money, yes an tu be wid yu.

BABS: I want to stay here. (*Pause.*) In fact, I'm not going back.

PASSION doesn't respond.

See it deh. Dat's why we cyarn work.

PASSION: Wait nuh. Tink me a tink… Ow yu garn live? Yu cyarn live on sunshine alone.

BABS: Well, how do you live?

PASSION: Only jus, me mek two an a half tousand J a week an mi pickney dem get half a dat.

BABS: That's (*Pause.*) damn, that's only thirty pounds. But you live, don't you? Me nah see you go hungry yet.

PASSION: (*Pauses, slightly uncomfortable.*) It nah easy.

BABS: Cynthia's done it.

PASSION: Cyntia yu falla? True yu tark Cyntia dis, Cyntia dat. Cyntia hav money.

BABS: Not as much as you all think. She borrowed the money for that land. Anyway I've made my mind up so you'll have to find another woman to send for you.

PASSION: Me nah wan no udda ooman. A yu me wan.

BABS: Don't wear all your lyrics out on me. You'll need them for later.

PASSION: (*With emphasis.*) Me say, a yu me wan.

BABS: You can't have it all, you have to decide, what do you want more?

PASSION: Me aready no.

Scene 10

Time has lapsed and the sun is about to set. ANISHA and RAS SIMI are walking downhill. RAS is carrying two black scandal bags and ANISHA is drinking a box drink.

RAS SIMI: Jah wid we, man.

ANISHA: I still can't believe it. My father, Pastor Brown, respected member of the community. He was a bus driver back in England, he hated it.

RAS SIMI: Si it deh, yard can wuk.

ANISHA: (*Smiles.*) It's like everyone knows everyone and when she said he had a photograph of me and my brothers, me (*Adopts accent.*) wid a coloured, square sinting a play wid, me nearly drop.

RAS SIMI: Yuh nevah tap being a fadda even if yu pickney nah dere fi call yu puppa.

ANISHA: Maybe he has other children now.

RAS SIMI: Maybe but he nah fahget bout yu.

ANISHA: Can you remember the directions? My heads in a spin.

RAS SIMI: Wha she say now, dun de ill an tun rite? Passion say dat, me tink him ketch a lucky guess.

ANISHA: And she said white house, verandah, tall grill…

RAS SIMI: Dere's a notice at the front too, may God go wid yu.

ANISHA: Oh yes. (*Stops walking.*) Simi? (*RAS stops too.*) I can't thank you enough for what you've done for me. If I hadn't met you, I'd probably still be hiding in complete denial. I know you haven't helped me because you have ulterior motives.

RAS SIMI's manner suggests the contrary but this appears to be done in jest.

I know you haven't, but I'd like you to carry me out one more time, if that's okay.

RAS SIMI: Yeah man, no problem. Where we a go?

ANISHA: The British High Commission. I'd love to help you get your visa so you can go and look for your sister.

RAS SIMI: Dats nice man. It would be good to see her yes but me nah really…

ANISHA: (*Cuts in.*) I'll take care of everything, I looked into it today. If we go soon (*Cautiously.*) you could take Babs' ticket and fly back with me.

RAS SIMI: Fa real?

ANISHA: I know what it's like to be separated from family.

RAS SIMI: Give thanx. Yu move fars man. If yuh nah get tru today, me still get fi go?

ANISHA: (*Laughing.*) Of course.

RAS SIMI: Blessings sistah. (*RAS SIMI embraces ANISHA and they both hold on a little too long. ANISHA looks a little embarrassed and they both start walking.*) Bwwoooy, me haffi pack up me khaki suit an me big boots dem, me no ow yuh Country love war aready. (*The moment has passed and they both laugh.*)

ANISHA: Is that your car?

RAS SIMI: Yeh man.

ANISHA: I can't hear any cussing.

RAS SIMI: Dem put up de window back.

ANISHA: Probably to keep the bugs out.

RAS SIMI: Yu hav de lime?

ANISHA: In my pocket.

RAS SIMI: Bumba. Yu see wha me a see?

They both stop in their tracks.

ANISHA: Me see it. So she and Passion done, is it? She's so full a shit.

RAS SIMI: We haffi go so… (*Looks at ANISHA.*) yu go call dem?

ANISHA: It's your car.

RAS SIMI: It nah look so. (*Pause.*) Fi yu fadda we a look fah.

ANISHA: He's your friend.

RAS SIMI: (*Pause.*) Me hav a idea. (*He pulls out his phone and begins to dial.*) Chuh, me credit done.

ANISHA: (*Lightly.*) Use mine. (*Hands over her phone.*)

RAS SIMI: (*Dials and waits.*) He nah answer.

ANISHA: He's engaged. Try again.

RAS SIMI redials PASSION's phone number.

If he don't answer this time we'll have to…

RAS SIMI: Wait nuh. (*Speaks in his best middle class Jamaican accent.*) Good hafternoon, this is Superintendent Adams. Passion dat? (*Pause.*) Don't get smart with me bwoy. I am placing you under arrest for bear nastiness and slack behaviour. Please get out of the vehicle with your hands up…

ANISHA: (*Whispers.*) Pants down.

RAS SIMI: …pants down and please put back the girl's brassiere.

ANISHA: (*Laughing.*) Tell him you're going to deport his dutty girlfriend.

RAS SIMI: Hush. (*Quietly.*) Him a tell she. (*Pause.*) Dem a laugh. (*Into phone.*) Me nah tell yu again bredrin.

PASSION and BABS appear, looking a bit dishevelled but thankfully fully clothed and are both laughing.

PASSION: (*With his hands in the air.*) Me guilty man.

BABS: (*Pointing at ANISHA.*) Don't you say a word.

ANISHA: My lips are sealed (*Pause.*) for now.

PASSION: Me need fi piss.

ANISHA: (*To BABS.*) Is that why his fly's down?

RAS SIMI: Me too. We soon come.

PASSION and RAS exit.

BABS: Dem two come like bench and batty.

ANISHA: (*Laughing.*) I leave you alone for five minutes…

BABS: Touche.

ANISHA: Here's the lime…rub it on anywhere that's sore.

BABS: Ha ha. How did you get on?

ANISHA: We know where we're going now so I give thanks for that and my father…

Phone rings interrupting ANISHA's speech.

ANISHA: It's not mine.

BABS: Passion must have left it… Shall I?

ANISHA: It might be Simi again, winding us up.

BABS picks up the phone.

BABS: Hello… (*In patois.*) Im busy right now, me him sista.

ANISHA: (*Mouths.*) What?

BABS: Right…say dat again…yeah man… (*Confused.*) …repeat…yes, no problem. (*Hangs up and is clearly fuming.*) The bastard.

ANISHA: Oh no.

BABS: (*Mocking voice, spoken in broken English.*) Why you tell him will be sending money for ticket, he needs telephone, telephone Liliana me and information give to him.

ANISHA: Ticket to where?

BABS: I didn't get his itinerary. Dutty johncrow.

ANISHA: They come from all over the world, looking Jamaican men. Didn't you say the Dancehall Queen was Japanese?

BABS: (*Overlapping and ignoring ANISHA's second point.*) Not for my rarted Jamaican man, they don't.

ANISHA: Sounds like you're not the only one with a back up plan.

BABS: Yeah but it looks like I'm his fucking plan B, little rars.

ANISHA: How thoughtless of him to meet her first.

BABS: You're supposed to be on my side.

ANISHA: I am but you shouldn't be so quick to condemn him, you're hardly a saint yourself. (*Imitating BABS.*) Doctor, can you check my blood pressure? I feel a little faint.

BABS: Between me and Cynthia, we could open a gigolo detection agency out here.

ANISHA: Yeah, call it Fool's Paradise or something like that.

BABS: Sounds about right.

ANISHA: I'll be your first client, find out if Simi is sincere.

BABS: You don't need a detective to work that out. Just because his friend's a ginal, doesn't make him one.

ANISHA: You don't know the full facts yet so don't jump to conclusions. The girl could barely speak English. (*Looks up to see if RAS SIMI and PASSION are approaching.*) They're coming back and I don't think this is the time or the place, if you know what I mean. Do you think you can hold it down?

BABS doesn't reply.

Babs?

Switch to PASSION and RAS SIMI's conversation. The conversation begins before they have finished their visit to the 'bathroom' and ends as they reach the girls. At first you can see the backs of them and it's clear from his actions that PASSION is having a little difficulty 'going'.

PASSION: So yu oo hav no intrest in goin ah foreign get tru, tu rars.

RAS SIMI: Jah nah gi yu wha yu wan, him gi yu wha yu need.

PASSION: Yeh? Well rite now me need sum bumba claat money. Me call de Italian gyal wen me deh pon me face lars week an she nah cum wid nutten. Now de Inglis one wan live a yard. Ow me bad lucky so?

RAS SIMI: Yu say yu nah wan nutten wid dat blonde gyal so wha yu a call ah fah?

PASSION: Chuh, me say me bruk man an she tell me she can get me a job an ting. Yu tark anyting wen yu belly a roll. Me nah inna anyting wid ah, a she want da anaconda. Me nah wine inna dat.

RAS SIMI: No bodda gi up lobster fah chicken back an dats cumin fram a ital man. Wha job she a go fine yu, cleaning up people dem shit? No sah. Lissen me, me wan gi yu me cyar fe run wen me a go up, mek yu control some serious US.

PASSION: Lang time since me operate a car.

RAS SIMI: Yu can mek wid one tour, wha yu mek in one week at dat place.

PASSION: Yu wud trus me wid yuh wheels?

RAS SIMI: Boss, me wud trus yu wid me life.

PASSION and RAS SIMI touch fists and acknowledge one another with a silent nod.

PASSION: Just say yu nah get tru, Babs might fine it 'ard yah an be ready fi fly home an me can still try a ting. Nah true?

RAS SIMI: Be positive man. Too much bad tinkin an we nah mek it. One one coco, full basket.

PASSION: Me jus a say if… Lickle more, me garn tark to ah again.

RAS SIMI: Member we deh pon a nex mission rite here now. Nah tek no argument to ah. Everyting will work out criss.

PASSION: Me jus a mek yu no wha gwarn. (*Shouts.*) Inglis, why yu two a tan up in de hot sun? (*To RAS SIMI.*) Dem crazy, yuh see.

The two men reach the girls and ANISHA watches BABS closely as she struggles to smile and act like nothing has happened.

BABS: You took your time. Did you relieve yourself in more ways than one?

PASSION: (*To BABS.*) Yu miss me baby? True, wen me nature rises, it 'ard fi go.

ANISHA: Spare us the detail…please.

RAS SIMI: (*Passes PASSION the car keys.*) Do yuh ting boss.

PASSION: (*Taken aback but recovers quickly.*) Yeh man, yeh man. (*Climbs into the driver's seat.*) Yeh man, straight.

RAS SIMI: (*To BABS.*) Yu a ride upfront.

ANISHA: She'll like that.

BABS throws ANISHA a look and climbs into the front passenger seat. RAS SIMI and ANISHA climb into the back.

(*To RAS.*) Can he drive a car?

RAS SIMI: No but him can fly plane.

ANISHA: I just wanna meet my father in this life, not the next.

PASSION: No bodda fret, yuh life safe in fi mi han.

BABS: (*Aside.*) But is your life safe in mine?

PASSION: Wha dat baby?

BABS: Nothing, honey. We trust you, don't we Nish?

ANISHA: Of course…like er…yeah, straight.

BABS: (*To PASSION.*) You okay, babe? (*Smiling.*) If even mosquito bite you, me fret.

PASSION: (*Smiling.*) I'm well criss man. Ras?

RAS SIMI: Blessed. (*To ANISHA.*) Yu ready Empress?

ANISHA: (*Smiles.*) Ready as I'll ever be, I guess.

RAS SIMI: Come den. (*Touches her hand.*) Let's fine de fadda.

PASSION turns on the engine, the stereo engages playing 'She's Been Loving Me' by Morgan Heritage and the play ends.